MUD, BLOOD
AND BULLETS

He asked, 'Is this the gun that's been firing all night?'

'Yes,' I said, 'Is anything wrong?'

'Far from it,' he replied. 'We've been out in front all night repairing the wire and the Jerries have been trying to sneak forward, throwing hand grenades. They couldn't quite reach us, thanks to your gun. Now there are seven of 'em lying on their own wire.'

I should have been delighted with this news, but I was not. I found I gained no satisfaction from it whatsoever; in fact, I was overcome by a feeling of deep remorse. 'Revenge is sweet' as the saying goes, but not for me. This may sound daft coming from a soldier on the front line of a war, but for the first time I felt like a murderer. All day I could not stop thinking about those seven men; men I had killed in revenge for my brother. Those men probably had brothers too, who would be mourning them, just as I was mourning Tom, and I had created another seven sad families.

CONTENTS

ACKNOWLEDGEMENTS

Firstly, my grateful thanks go to the members of the Machine Gun Corps Old Comrades Association, who continue to work so hard to keep and honour the memory of the 170,000 men who served in the Machine Gun Corps from 1915–1922. I would especially like to thank Graham Sacker, Judith Lappin and Andy Bray for their help, and for welcoming me so warmly as a new 'Old Comrade'. I am also indebted to Bill Fulton of the Machine Gun Corps History Project, and his colleague Phil McCarty, for their generous assistance and unfailing patience in answering my many email queries.

I owe a huge debt of gratitude to Shaun Barrington at The History Press, for his belief that these memoirs were worthy of a 'proper' publisher, and to my editor Miranda Jewess for her help and support. Also, if I may, I would like to say an enormous thank you to my lovely, long-suffering husband Graham, who has spent these past months covering all the jobs on the Home Front while his wife has been 'living' in the trenches of the Western Front. Thank you also to family members who scoured their attics for photos, especially Chris Hill and Graham Foxall.

Lastly, and most importantly of all, I want to thank my mother, Edward Rowbotham's much-loved daughter, who not only gave her permission for me to take away and edit Grandad's notes and memoirs, but regularly sat uncomplaining while I ransacked her sideboards and cupboards in search of medals, family mementoes and old photographs.

INTRODUCTION

The Great War, the one that was supposed to 'end all wars' but, of course, did not, has a unique place in British history. We remain fascinated by it – even 90 years on. We remember it because of the sheer numbers of young British men who fought in it for their country – more than in any other war either before or since – and the fact that many of these men did not belong to the regular army but were volunteers and conscripts. We also remember it for the dreadful toll of the slaughter of these young men; by the time of the Armistice in 1918 nearly a million of them were dead or missing, and around another million wounded. Edward Rowbotham, my grandfather, was one of the volunteers.

What life was like for the common soldier on the front line during the four years the war raged has, of course, been documented; however, most of the literature – books, memoirs, diaries – have been written by academics, politicians and officers, people who did not experience the war from quite the same perspective as the rank and file. There have been comparatively few detailed first-hand accounts written by the common soldier.

People born into the generation who could remember the First World War are gone now, and gone with them is the likelihood of obtaining any more first-hand accounts – which makes my grandfather's memoirs a precious piece of history, possibly one of the final first-hand accounts to be discovered.

Edward Rowbotham was born in 1890, one of fourteen children from a working-class family in the Black Country at the end of the Victorian era. Although the Rowbothams were a loving and close family, there were so many mouths to feed that Grandad was no stranger to hardship and deprivation as he was growing up. He was a young man of 24, a coal miner, at the time Britain declared war on Germany. From the start he was desperate to join up, but he was by that time one of the principal breadwinners in the family and couldn't be spared. Lord Kitchener kept pointing to him personally from the posters, telling him his country needed him, but he didn't need telling; he truly wanted to be a hero, a 'glory boy', as he called it. He finally enlisted in November 1915, proud to accept the King's Shilling and become one of Kitchener's Army. Even when he realised, too late, that he had volunteered himself to fight at the very gates of hell, his sense of duty never faltered. He would see it through without complaint. 'I just got on with it and made the best of things,' he would always say about it afterwards with typical understatement.

He enlisted as a private in November 1915, joining the 5th South Staffordshire Regiment, but from there he was drafted into the newly-formed Machine Gun Corps and sent to the Western Front. There, he fought in every major conflict from March 1916 onwards, at Ypres and on the Somme. Men of the Machine Gun Corps, specially trained in the operation of the Vickers light automatic machine gun, were always deployed on the front line of the battlefield, sometimes even ahead of it in no-man's-land, and sitting targets for every weapon the enemy could throw at them; so much so that members were sometimes known as 'the suicide club'. Casualties, inevitably, were enormous. Of the 170,000 officers and men who served in the Machine Gun Corps, 62,000 of them became casualties (over 36 per cent): of these, nearly 14,000 were killed, and a further 48,000 were wounded, missing or prisoners of war. Edward Rowbotham was extremely lucky to be one of the survivors.

Uncomplaining, he endured the horrors and the brutal hardships of the trenches, his courage, stoicism and good humour seeing him through the darkest times. His passion for life never left him – there were even times when he actually seemed to *enjoy* the war. As a soldier he fought bravely and did his duty, which was to kill as many of the enemy as he could, but he was essentially a kind and gentle man. He had enormous compassion for his fellow man, on one occasion risking his own life to rescue, under enemy fire, one of his gun team, mortally injured in no-man's-land, so that his comrade would not be left to die in a shell hole (every soldier's dread) – an act for which he was awarded the Military Medal.

He wrote these memoirs in 1967, 50 years after the war, and yet he describes life in the trenches so vividly, as if the events had happened to him only yesterday. An enthusiastic storyteller, with excellent powers of recall, he had an amazing capacity for bringing his experiences to life. The stories he recounts I heard as a child many times (I adored him, my lovely brave Grandad, and I loved to listen to his tales of heroic deeds) and this helped me to edit his memoirs with confidence, enabling me to clarify the odd point where necessary, even adding the occasional titbit of information, which, for whatever reason, he omitted from his written account.

I know he wouldn't mind a bit that I have changed his title. He gave his book the title *Memoirs of a Plebeian*. He described himself as a 'plebeian', meaning an ordinary working man, but there was nothing ordinary about him at all. He was a funny, articulate, highly intelligent man, who happened to be born into the lower classes at a time when it was almost impossible to move up. Opportunities were simply not there for him; had he been born today, I am certain he would have gone to university (Oxford probably, as his great grandson did a century later) and he would have had a good career, earning the kind of money Grandad spent his life hoping for, but never found.

Why it has taken over 40 years to approach a publisher with these remarkable reminiscences is a mystery. After he completed his memoirs (all painstakingly handwritten on foolscap paper and 'professionally' glued into a home-made binder, with the title on the front improvised from letters cut out of the *Daily Mirror*) Grandad passed it round the many and various members of the Rowbotham clan, and we all read it. I was only twelve at the time, and although I was given them to read I was still too young to really appreciate their importance.

After Grandad died in 1973, 'The Book', as he called it, was put away in Mum's sideboard along with other treasured family keepsakes, like his Military Medal. Then, around the times of the 90th anniversaries of the battles of the Somme and Passchendaele, there seemed to be renewed media interest in the First World War, with books and TV programmes and many articles appearing in the newspapers. Mum remarked to me, 'Your Grandad fought in the Battle of the Somme, and at Passchendaele – *and* he managed to come home in one piece at the end of it. He wrote about it all in 'The Book'.'

Of course he did! I took out 'The Book' and began to read it again. It didn't take me long to realise that it was more than just a family memoir, it was an important piece of history: a detailed and fascinating first-hand account of an ordinary soldier's experiences of the Great War. I was determined to see if I could get it published for him.

So, here they are: my Grandad's memoirs, lovingly revised and edited by his granddaughter. I have two regrets. The first is that he is not here to see 'The Book' in print (he would have been so proud); the second that he is not here to answer the very many questions I desperately want to ask him about his extraordinary life. But then, as Grandad always used to say, 'You can't have everything, can you?'

He dedicated his memoirs to his daughter and grandchildren; now I feel very proud indeed to dedicate them to his memory.

This is his story.

Janet Tucker

FOREWORD TO THE
ORIGINAL MANUSCRIPT
MEMOIRS OF A PLEBEIAN

When I decided to write my memoirs I had two objects in view: firstly, to occupy my time in retirement, and secondly, to provide a record of events of my own lifetime, indicating the way of life enjoyed (I use that word loosely) by my generation of working class people.

I have wondered many times what life was like in my father's and grandfather's times. So, I propose to set down something of my life and times on the assumption that my grandchildren and their grandchildren in turn might wish to know what life was like for an ordinary working class lad growing up in the Black Country in late Victorian and Edwardian times; and then, as a young man, going to fight for his country on the bloody battlefields of the Western Front; then afterwards, on returning to normal life, how he coped (I use that word loosely too) with the aftermath of war.

I have called myself a 'plebeian' rather than a 'working man' because almost every man calls himself a working man and I wish to confine my observations to the class of people who have to work in order to live; in other words the Common Man.

Much has been written about the Great War, but the accent has invariably been on the exploits and habits of people in high places –

the politicians, generals and officers. Not so much has been written from the viewpoint of the common man. These memoirs represent that point of view, and they are a true record of my own life.

Edward Rowbotham, 1967

CHAPTER ONE

A WORKING CLASS LAD

I was born in the year 1890, the seventh child of a family of fourteen (fifteen if you count a twin who died at two months). My brothers and sisters were, from the eldest down, Harry, Len, Albert, Ernie, Ada, Edie, Me, Gertie, Tom, Edgar, Hilda, Nellie, Frank and George. At the time of my birth we lived in a small terraced house in Reeves Street, Bloxwich, in the Midlands.

My dad was a hard-working man and loved his family. He was a coal miner and good enough at his job to earn as much money as the next man, though that was little enough in all conscience. He liked his drink of beer, but only imbibed when he could afford it. He never went to school, so could not read or write – but he had the intelligence to actually teach himself to read once he was forced to give up work when he was only 50 through ill health brought about by the abominable conditions which prevailed in the pits in the Midlands at the time.

The pits were grim, most of them wet and damp, and often men would be working all day in water over their boot-tops. Ventilation was so bad that, more often than not, the air was polluted, filled with powder smoke from the blasting operations. Not many men of my dad's generation continued to work after the age of 50 or so. Penal servitude would have seemed like a holiday to them; after all, the convicts at least had fresh air to breathe.

My mother, bless her, was a fount of wisdom and knowledge, and 'Mother Confessor' not only to her family but to her friends and relations as well. Not only that, she could read and write, no mean achievement for her generation. She possessed a fine sense of humour – she needed it with fourteen children – and the family was a happy one. We were devastated when she died at the age of 55, and it seemed to us ironic that she should be taken just at the time she could have started to enjoy her grown-up family. My sisters, Ada and Edie had to take over the responsibilities of the household, assisted by Dad, who was practically an invalid himself by then, although he lived to be 71.

We were a close-knit family, but as I look back now I realise what an immense struggle it must have been to raise our mob. There were already nine children before the first one, Harry, was old enough to go out to work. It is hard to imagine now what it must have been like with a house full of kids and only one worker to support us all. The burden of the household duties fell on my mother. She worked day and night to keep us fed and clothed, proud that she managed it without ever having to apply for Parish Relief. Parish Relief was only one step short of the shame of being sent to the workhouse – an ever-present threat to large families.

Many families where the father couldn't, or didn't want to work, or was not very good at managing the household finances, or he spent too much of the household finances in the pub, would end up in the workhouse. The workhouse was a wretched place, where the family would be subject to humiliating conditions. Charles Dickens wasn't exaggerating.

By the grace of God we never reached that stage, and it was my parents' proud and justifiable boast that none of their children had ever gone to bed hungry. On the contrary, we considered ourselves well-fed. Mother baked all our own bread. She baked once a week, enough bread to last until the following week, and when the day's fragrant baking was piled on the table, anyone who didn't know us would have thought we were preparing for a siege. The highlight of baking day, to us children at least, was the time for the removal from the oven of the flap-jacks, which, when cooked, were about six inches in diameter and about an inch and a half thick. Mother would give us one each while they were still hot, and we would separate them and put in a slice of cheese or a knob of butter. The heat would melt the filling and they were delicious!

It was an awe-inspiring sight to see the family at meal times, particularly at Sunday dinner, when we were all round the table. The size of the meat joint would make some of the offerings you see in shops today look very puny indeed. In winter the evenings would be spent talking about pit-work, Dad and the elder brothers discussing the day's happenings down the pit, what they said to the 'gaffer' or what the 'gaffer' had said to them or, when Len was at home, listening to him play the organ. Mother would be darning socks, or making a dress or pair of trousers for one of us, the girls washing up or tidying a room, the younger ones playing Ludo or draughts or snakes and ladders. Then Dad would say 'Come on, that's enough, let's 'ave yer up the wooden hill!', and Mother, assisted by my sisters, would prepare the younger ones for bed, and, when all the children had gone up, it was suddenly very peaceful.

Sunday evenings were the highlight of the week. Len would be at the organ, and the family would gather round singing hymns with such gusto that often there would be quite a crowd gathered outside our front window. Although we weren't church-goers it was a strict rule that only hymns should be sung on Sundays. Len offered to give me lessons on the organ as I was so keen on playing it, but alas, after about six lessons he started courting a young girl, so it is easy to guess what happened to my music tuition after that. Nevertheless, I kept on practising, and I was so eager to play that practically all my spare time was spent at the organ. Although I couldn't read music, I eventually taught myself to play quite a number of tunes by ear; in fact, I progressed well enough to deputise for Len at our Sunday sing-songs when he was absent.

Our house around this period was hardly ever without visitors. Friends of my older brothers or my Dad would come to have a look at the pigs we kept in the yard, or to discuss their work in the pit. At weekends, particularly on a Sunday morning, we always had visitors and the parlour would be thick with tobacco smoke, and the conversation would be about – guess what? Pit work! I think my mother and sisters could have worked a coal mine; they heard so much about pit work they could give a competent message in detail to one of the night shift from one of the day shift.

One visitor, Tom Holden, who was one of Albert's pals, bought a new gramophone, an Edison (which as a cylindrical type should have been called a phonograph, but we called them all gramophones). It was his very proud possession. We prevailed on Tom to bring it round, and the first time he brought it we were enraptured and mystified as to how a person's voice could be made to come up a little trumpet like that. The records were cylindrical and cost sixpence each. The general verdict was 'whatever will they think of next?'

Seeing the new gramophone and how it worked solved a mystery for me, for I had actually seen and heard one some time before at Leamore Flower Show. It was up on a platform with the gramophone itself resting on a large box. We were all eagerly waiting for the gramophone recital to start and when it did we were flabbergasted to hear a man's voice coming up through the trumpet. We couldn't believe it and thought somebody was having us on. We were convinced they had a man hiding in the box underneath, singing the songs.

CHAPTER TWO

SCHOOL DAYS –
QUEEN VICTORIA'S JUBILEE

Life at school was no bed of roses. The teachers wielded the cane far too frequently and it was little consolation to us when our elders told us how lucky we were to be getting a free education and that 'we didn't know we were born …' Inwardly, I thought it was they who were the lucky ones, not having to go to school.

Out of school hours, of course, we were much the same as any other generation of kids – noisy, mischievous and full of the joy of life. And the best part of school, naturally, was the holidays.

Bloxwich Wake, the annual fair and one of the highlights of our year, always came in the August holidays. The excitement would mount as the Wake ground began to fill up with caravans and all the paraphernalia of the side-shows, coconut shies etc, all horse-drawn. Most of the big attractions, such as the gondolas, the mounting ponies, the steam boat and Pat Collins' own big show were drawn by a huge steam traction engine which operated between the Wake ground and Bloxwich railway station, where it would arrive on flat trucks. This is where us kids came in. One of the workmen would put a megaphone to his mouth and bawl out, 'Come on lads, down to the railway station and help unload the trucks!' We would be promised free admission to the Wake in return for our labours, so down to the station we would race, hundreds of us it would seem.

The workmen would attach a thick heavy rope to whatever it was to be unloaded, while the kids would be positioned along the length of the rope, one each side alternately. And then we would start to pull. The first pull would be from the siding to the gates, and a second pull would move the object up onto the road so that the traction engine could be hooked up to it. When there were enough objects hooked up to the traction engine it would haul them all up to the Wake ground, while another 'train' of stuff was hauled into position by kid-power. Those wake folk certainly knew what they were doing, using us kids as a free haulage machine. Of course, we were under the fond delusion that they would keep their promise to let us in for free (admission was 2*d* for adults and 1*d* for children), but when our work was done we were not even allowed to stay in the ground to watch the roundabouts assembled; as soon as the last load was hauled in from the station they would round us all up one last time and tell us to clear off, much to our disappointment.

'We won't 'elp ya next year. You can pull the rope yourselves,' we would plead, but to no avail.

'Gerroff!' would be their final word on the matter.

A year is a long time in a youngster's life, however, and by the time the Wake came round again it was forgotten and we would fall for the same trick all over again.

While I was still very young I saw, with others, a phenomenon which I have not seen since that time and have often wondered if I could have dreamt the whole thing, and if I told the story so many times that I had come to believe it myself. It was summer and the morning was sultry and close, and shortly before we were to be let out of school for the lunch break, a heavy thunderstorm broke. It was so severe that we were kept in school until it abated. When we were eventually let out, the water was gushing down the street gutters and almost overwhelming the drains and, like boys of all generations, we rushed to paddle in it. To our amazement we found that there were hundreds of little silver col-oured fish in the water, not more than about half an inch long. As the water receded they were left high and dry and flapping about all over the place. At the end of afternoon school, we returned to look for the fish and found the poor things lying in the gutters – all dead.

I have, during the course of my 77 years, told this story many times to many different people. Sometimes I have been believed, but at other times I have sensed a certain disbelief, never openly contradicted, but just a wry smile perhaps, or a doubtful glance. When I decided to write these memoirs, I thought I would try to have the story verified, or otherwise, by writing to the BBC Weather Unit – and I received this reply:

Room 4095

Weather Unit

BBC

1st April 1967

Dear Mr Rowbotham

Thank you for your letter. The event you mention is certainly possible meteorologically speaking. When violent, thundery conditions exist, there is also a tendency for water-spouts and whirlwinds to form locally. In the case you describe, water from a pool or lake could have been sucked up into the clouds, and the whole lot, water, fishes and all, dropped some distance away.

Mind you, this does not happen frequently, although one or two similar occurrences have been reported from various places.

Yours sincerely

P.H. Walker

Well, fancy that!

There is another incident from my school days that I think is worth recording, particularly in view of all the stress we seem to lay on hygiene these days. I refer to the Christmas 'Scrum'. This was when sweets were given out to the children before breaking up for the Christmas holidays. Now, whether the teachers did it this way for the children's benefit or for their own malicious enjoyment we never knew, but instead of giving every child a few sweets each, which would have been the fairer way, one of the big classrooms would be cleared of desks. Whether the floor was swept I do not remember, and at that age I probably didn't care. All the children, large and small, would be assembled in the classroom. Then, the teachers would come in carrying huge bags of sweets and start throwing the sweets up into the air, trying to reach all four corners of the room so that everyone would have a 'fair' chance of getting some. Well, the noise can be better imagined than described, and it was definitely a case of survival of the fittest, the oldest and the tallest, as the big boys pushed the little ones aside and grabbed the lion's share.

Some boys – it always seemed to be the same ones – ended up with their pockets bulging, while the smaller boys got just a few. The teachers always appeared to be having the time of their lives. Wrapped sweets were unknown in those days and often the sweets were retrieved from the floor covered in dust and bits of fluff. The teachers would tell us, 'You have to eat a peck of dirt before you die', and, thinking about those Christmas scrums, I suppose we must have done.

I was seven years old in 1897 and attending Leamore School at the time of Queen Victoria's Diamond Jubilee, the greatest occasion of my young life. Flags and banners, bunting and garlands festooned every building, it seemed. Everywhere was covered in red, white and blue and everyone wore some kind of emblem, a rosette, a hat-band, or bits of ribbon in their caps. It was a red, white and blue world. In some shop windows there were framed pictures of Queen Victoria and Prince Albert (who had died many years before). All this to me looked like fairyland. I had never seen anything like it before and it was wonderful to be alive.

Since then, of course, there have been many occasions when the town has become red, white and blue again – the coronations of Edward VII, George V, George VI, Elizabeth II; and also the victories in two world wars – but none ever impressed me as profoundly as Queen Victoria's Diamond Jubilee.

For me, the culmination of the festivities was the school party. We kids all wore our best clothes, including the old-fashioned schoolboy's collar. Our shoes were blacked and our hands and faces washed. We wore ribbons, red, white and blue, of course, round our necks, suspended from which was a tea cup, which swung at waist level.

This was one of those rare occasions when attending school was a real pleasure. We sat in our places, our cups, still attached to the long ribbons, on the desks, and we were waited on by the teachers. One teacher poured the tea, another gave us a paper bag containing cakes and sweets, while other teachers hovered around like guardian angels with trousers on. Being waited on by our natural enemy, *and* allowed to talk in class, was almost unbelievable. We finished the day by singing patriotic songs with one of the teachers at the piano, and conducted by the headmaster, ending with the National Anthem which we sang with great gusto. How we wished that Queen Victoria would have a jubilee every week!

But, as the saying goes, 'After the Lord Mayor's Show comes the dustcart', and sadly, the next day, school was as usual, all the bunting and flags taken down and the carnival spirit gone. We were all rather depressed. But, such is the resilience of youth – we soon got over it and started looking forward to the next binge, which was the Sunday School treat, when we would have tea and cakes again.

I shall always remember the Jubilee as one of the happiest episodes of my young life. There are others, of course, which I shall come to later, but this was the very first, hence the memorable impact.

School, generally, was hard and the teachers strict, with beatings a regular part of the school day. A few years after the Jubilee, I had an experience with Mr Satterthwaite, the headmaster of Bloxwich National School that I did not enjoy one bit.

My mother kept me at home on the Monday morning to mind the babies, as it was her custom to keep one of us, in turn, every Monday morning. It was my turn on this particular Monday, not that I minded, as a note from Mother to the teacher on my return to school would usually excuse me from punishment. Monday, of course, was washing day, and this was the age before washing machines, when washing clothes for a large family like ours was a major operation. So, the teachers were usually sympathetic to children kept at home on washdays.

Unlucky for me, however, the headmaster had decided on this particular Monday to take over the punishment of absentees himself, and
duly instructed the teachers to send the morning absentees to him.
I was among them. The queue reached from the headmaster's desk
right through into the next classroom – there must have been 40 or 50
of us. I was about half-way down the queue and could see quite clearly
what was happening up at the front and I was not at all happy about it.
Mr Satterthwaite, an unsmiling man at the best of times, was looking
particularly grim on this occasion, and it boded ill for us.

'Where were you this morning?' I heard him ask the first boy.

'Please, Sir,' replied the boy, 'I had to stay at home to mind the baby.
I have a note from my mother, Sir.'

Ignoring the note, the headmaster thundered, 'Hold out your hand,'
and the cane came down with a mighty swish (he always aimed at the
tips of the fingers where the pain would be greatest), 'Now the other
one,' and again that horrible swish.

Boy after boy received the same treatment until he came to a boy,
three in front of me. He was one of the 'rich kids' and the headmaster's
attitude changed instantly.

'And why weren't you at school this morning, John?' he asked, quite
pleasantly.

'Please, Sir, I had to go to Walsall to fetch my new bicycle.'

'Oh, I see, alright then,' said the headmaster. 'Get on to your class.'

Being so close, I heard it all, and I had an idea. The punishments
continued. The next two boys, despite having notes from their moth-
ers, got the cane. As my turn came, although I still had the note from
Mother in my pocket, I had decided not to use it.

'And why didn't *you* come to school this morning, Rowbotham?'
the headmaster asked me sternly.

'Please, Sir, I had to go to Walsall to fetch my new bicycle,' I said.

He knew, of course, that I could not afford a packet of pins much less
a new bicycle.

'Right!' he growled. 'Hold out your hand.' Wallop. 'Now the other.'
Wallop. 'That's two,' he said. 'Now I am going to give you two more for

telling lies.' And he did too – and I couldn't think why my bright idea had gone so wrong.

When I got home from school that evening and told Mother and the family what had happened, they thought it was very funny, but, believe me, I couldn't see the joke. Now I look back on the incident, I suppose it was the same as a boy of today saying to their teacher, 'Please, Sir, I had to go to Walsall to pick up my new Rolls Royce.'

I was about twelve when the following incidents took place. We had by then left Reeves Street, Bloxwich, where my early childhood was spent, to 129 Green Lane, Leamore, known as The Quadrant. It was one of a row of eight houses opposite the Four Crosses pub. We thought we had gone up in the world. Each house contained a modern cooking range, a private wash-house (or brew-house, 'brewuss' as it was called) and, a great luxury, a private toilet across the blue-brick yard. This was our first experience of a 'water closet', although it still didn't have the convenience of a flushing tank, and we had to carry a bucket of water across the yard for flushing. Still, it was a vast improvement on the old 'earth closet' at Reeves Street, and I remember how wonderful it felt for me, as a young lad, to sit on a toilet without fear of falling down the hole. Now, this may sound comical, but there was nothing to laugh at about an earth closet and its accompanying ash-pit, middings or bog-hole. In a nutshell, the earth closet was an abomination and when we left Reeves Street I hoped I would never have to see, use or smell one again; little did I know that a few years later I would have to endure 'facilities' much worse than the earth closet, when I was in the trenches on the Western Front.

The Quadrant also had the benefit of gas laid on. After the dim lighting we were used to, from our paraffin lamps and candles, the much brighter light provided by the new gas mantles seemed, by comparison, of such brilliance that my father used to exclaim that it 'beat daylight into fits'. There was a gas cooker too, but in those early days of gas, there was a widespread suspicion that the gas would contaminate the food being cooked, so my mother continued to use the old coal fire and oven. We just used the gas ring to boil the kettle.

Often, on Saturday afternoons, one or other of my elder brothers would need a cap, a pair of socks or perhaps a tie from a shop next door to the Crown Inn in Leamore Lane. The shop was kept by Mr Sam Lidgett. Whenever I went in his shop he would invariably ask me to spell something. On the day of this story, there was a commercial traveller in his shop and, when I entered, Mr Lidgett said to the other man, 'Now, here's a bright lad. Ask him to spell something.'

'Alright,' said the man. 'Spell Zulu.'

'Z-U-L-U,' said I.

'What did I tell you!' said Mr Lidgett.

'Very good indeed,' said the other man.

Little did I know I was being conned. The commercial traveller said he needed a bright lad, then asked me if I would do something for him and he would pay me well. I agreed of course. He said he wanted me to carry his two suitcases of samples to two houses in Harden Road, which was just round the corner. That little chore would be easy, I thought. I was a sturdy lad and the cases didn't seem too heavy. So, off we went. We called at the two houses and then he told me there were two more just up the road.

'We won't be long,' he said.

There were just two more houses, then two more, then two more, until we had been all round Goscote and Blakenall, during which time he never touched the cases except to go into each house with them. By this time, apart from the cases weighing about a ton each and growing heavier by the minute, I was very worried about what was going to happen to me when I finally reached home – a good hiding for sure. Eventually, we came down Blakenall Lane, to the tram terminus at Leamore Lane. There he told me to put the cases on the waiting tram, then he put his hand in his pocket and took out tuppence, which he gave me. Then he got on the tram to Walsall without another word.

I was thankful to be rid of those suitcases and very pleased with my reward, and had it not been for the grim foreboding of a hiding waiting for me, I would have felt happy despite my near exhaustion. I must say here that when any of us had a hiding from Mother it was always well-deserved, and she would always hear our story first – before tanning our backsides.

So it was on this occasion. I didn't have to make up a story, as Mother could see I was about all in, and she was so sympathetic that I began to cry.

'Wait till I see that Sam Lidgett,' she said. 'I'll give him a piece of my mind.'

As a thank-you offering for my reprieve I insisted on Mother taking a penny of my two pence 'wages'. Tuppence, to me, seemed a small fortune when our weekly pocket money was only a halfpenny. You could get quite a lot of things for a halfpenny in those days. Usually, we went in for quantity rather than quality, like a lucky bag, a bag of tiger nuts, or perhaps a pomegranate. Once the choice had been made (and this might take some time) that was it until the next week, except for an odd one or two sweets from a packet we would share which came with the box of groceries on a Saturday.

I remember one Saturday when I had bought a lucky bag I found inside it an exact replica of a silver threepenny bit, made in cardboard. It was exact in every detail. Oh, if this was only real, I thought, and, in consultation with my bosom pal, George Keeling, decided to wait till it was dark and then go to Bloxwich and try to exchange it for real money. Dame Fortune smiled upon us in the shape of a paper-seller named Dodd, who was a cripple. We went up to him and asked him to change a threepenny bit. He agreed cheerfully and counted three pennies into my hand.

I put my cardboard threepenny bit into his hand quickly, then we dashed off like a pair of scalded cats, down the side street and back to Leamore. We shared the threepence, and with so much money to spend we ought to have been very happy boys, but I fear we were not. I do not remember exactly what we did with the money but I *do* remember that we did not enjoy the fruits of our labours, due undoubtedly to a pair of guilty consciences.

Some years later, however, when I was working, and receiving half a crown a week pocket money, I was in the Coffee House, Parkside, Bloxwich, where young people used to gather to play bagatelle and drink coffee, and who should come in but Dodd. He didn't know me but I knew him. My conscience had troubled me many times since I had tricked him and I had inwardly decided that if I ever had the opportunity to pay him back I would do so. Now was my opportunity, and when Mr Dodd had settled down I went over to him and asked him if he remembered me.

'No. I don't think I know ya,' he said. I reminded him of the episode with the threepenny bit.

'Now do you remember me?' I asked.

'Oh, I do now. There was two of ya.'

'That's right,' I said.

'Well, well,' he said with a smile. 'Fancy that after all this time. If I could of catched ya I would have tanned yer behinds.'

'I want to pay you back now, Mr Dodd. Do you think a tanner will square it?'

'Go on with ya. I don't want nothing,' he said uncomfortably.

I pressed the sixpence into his hand and bought him a cup of coffee as well. He seemed very well satisfied and at last my conscience was clear.

It was very rare indeed in Edwardian times for a working class man to be measured for a new suit and pay for it with ready cash; instead, we had someone called the 'Packman', who called every week to collect instalments of between sixpence and a shilling towards a new suit (which cost around £2 to £3, according to the quality desired). Younger children seldom had new clothes; they had to be content with 'hand-me-downs'. However, it must be said that only the very poorest folk did not possess a Sunday suit or dress. Sunday was always a special day when everyone wore their very best clothes – even if those clothes spent the remainder of the week reposing in the pawnshop. The Packman gave a good service and the clothes he sold us were always well cut, and they lasted well enough to be handed down to the next in line.

Although we were a very happy and close family, the standard of living we 'enjoyed' was very poor in comparison to today, but, compared with our parents' living standards in Victorian England, we were told we were lucky to be born into such enlightened times. While our parents had no schooling, we had free, compulsory education, so practically all my generation of working class children could read and write. However, enlightened times or not, there were almost no opportunities for anyone from this newly educated lower class to 'move up'. My father and older brothers were all miners, and I knew that pit-work was my future too, although I always yearned for something better.

There was always a regular wage coming into the house, but we were far from wealthy; coal miners at that time earned a fairly meagre wage of less than ten shillings a week. The rent on a typical terraced house could be anything from two and sixpence a week to ten shillings a week, depending on the number of bedrooms it had. Our house in Church Street, Bloxwich, which we moved to when I was in my early teens, had four bedrooms to accommodate our large family, and had a rent of ten shillings a week.

To give an insight into the cost of living around the turn of the century, I can still recall the price of a few commodities around that time. I do not pretend to remember the price of everything but if I give a few of those I do remember it may give an idea.

Daily newspapers   ½d
Sunday newspapers   1d
Five cigarettes   1d
Twist tobacco   3d per ounce
Beer   3d per pint
Whisky 3/6 per bottle
Tarragona Port Wine   1/- per quart bottle
Sausages   6d per pound
Meat   4d–6d per pound
Butter   5d–6d per pound
Eggs   1d each
Caps, socks, ties –6½d average

On Sunday nights, all publicans would give each customer a clay pipe and half an ounce of twist tobacco free. If not a pipe smoker, the customer would receive a packet of cigarettes. On weekdays, however, if someone wanted a clay pipe it would cost a halfpenny.

My mother would always shop for bargains. If you were lucky and got in early at the cake shop on Monday mornings, a large paper bagful of stale cakes from Saturday could be obtained for a penny. We never minded how stale they were, we enjoyed them anyway. I often wonder what happens to stale cakes these days.

There were no domestic refrigerators at this time and I don't know of any local shop that had one either. Consequently, the best bargains were to be had a little before closing time on Saturday nights. The butchers, fishmongers, and all the purveyors of perishable goods had to clear out their stocks, especially in summer, for the weekend. In addition to the stale cakes, we could also go to almost any fruit shop and buy a 'ha'porth of specked fruit'. On some occasions we could take our little wagon (a soap box on two pram wheels) and get it filled with all kinds of fruit. We would sort out the best of it for eating and feed the rest to the pigs. We were seldom without a pig, sometimes two. In fact, there were very few miners who didn't have a pig in the sty in the yard – it was the custom in those parts.

CHAPTER THREE

THE BOER WAR –
WORKING LIFE

In 1899 the Boer War broke out. I was nine years old and I can remember being shown on a map at school where South Africa was. Many people had never heard of the place. As far as I or any of my contemporaries were concerned though, this war was a big new game. We had mock battles in the school playground, and all of us wore an emblem bearing the picture of our favourite general. My favourite was General Baden-Powell. He looked so dashing in his colonial, wide-brimmed hat, slightly tilted (this, of course, was the man who later went on to found the Boy Scouts in 1907). My second favourite was General Sir Redvers Buller, who, according to the consensus of opinion among our elders, had a raw deal at Ladysmith, and the credit for relieving Ladysmith, which had been besieged by the Boers for some time, was given to Field Marshal Lord Roberts. Though the relief of Ladysmith was an occasion for national rejoicing, it was felt by the public that Sir Redvers Buller had stoutly defended the town with an inadequate force, and then Lord Roberts had come along with an overwhelming force of men, marched into the town and then received all the credit. Whatever the rights and wrongs of this case, I do not pretend to know. I was too young to have an opinion except to absorb the thinking of my elders.

It was rather odd though that little was heard of Buller after that while Roberts was boosted in the press – but we kids still wore the emblem of Buller. Perhaps we were wrong, or rather our elders were, because Lord Roberts went on to win the Victoria Cross, and it can never be said that any soldier ever won that great trophy unless he had performed exceptionally brave deeds. Nevertheless, it was Baden Powell who was our idol, more especially when he brought about the relief of Mafeking in 1900. This event brought out the flags and banners; the siege of Mafeking had been a long and bitter struggle.

I recall finding a piece of wood, by strange coincidence, shaped exactly like a miniature rifle. It became my most cherished possession, and I took it with me wherever I went, except to school, where it would have had a very short life. I kept it in a secret place at home; I took it with me on errands; took part in battles with it; did imitation drills with it; and rubbed and polished it with as much pride as if it were real. What a soldier I was! I shot thousands of imaginary Boers with it, and no soldier was ever more proud of a rifle than I was of that piece of wood. It's a wonder Baden Powell didn't give me a medal.

I remember well the death of Queen Victoria in 1901. The Boer War had been raging then for two years, and it was said in the press that it had hastened her end. She had reigned for 64 years and none of our elders had known any other sovereign but Victoria. I recall there was a lot of talk and some speculation as to what sort of a king Edward VII would turn out to be, bearing in mind the stories in our history books of the cruel monarchs of the past. I was only eleven at this time and wondered whether our new king would have people beheaded as King Henry VIII did! I need not have worried. King Edward VII became widely known as Edward the Peacemaker, and life in what was now Edwardian England went on much as before.

The Boer War ended in 1902 amid great rejoicing. Everyone feted the soldiers when they returned; this was something new and meant that the soldier had finally come into his own. Up to the outbreak of the Boer War, the soldier belonged to the lowest stratum of society. It was generally considered that the British Army was composed mainly of social misfits, ex-jail birds, and men running away from their domestic responsibilities. It may have been true in some cases, but it is hard to believe now that it was true in every case – such was public opinion.

School leaving age was fourteen, but parents could take their children away at thirteen under certain circumstances. It was only in 1900 that the minimum age for coalminers had been raised from twelve to thirteen. I was able to leave school at thirteen provided I could get a job, but it was not to be, for I wandered around the town for five months without success. So, I had to return to school for another seven months, much to my disgust.

As it was possible to go to any school of your choice in the borough, I chose not to go back to the National School and to go to the Roman Catholic school in Harrison Street in Bloxwich instead, because, I thought, as they had female teachers they would be more lenient with the cane. Not so! I found out very quickly that the fair sex could be just as cruel as men. Some of the boys would cry after a caning, but I was determined that I would never cry. I thought, 'there is only one woman who can make *me* cry and that's my mother.'

Fortunately, I was only at the school for seven months and was quite a big boy by then. Had I been there throughout my schooldays it is doubtful whether I could have kept my vow not to cry, but keep it I did, and eventually my birthday arrived. So, at the tender age of fourteen I had to find myself a job. Some of the bigger lads who worked at the local brickyard (Leamore Brick Co.) advised me to just go into the brickyard and help out in the hope that when the gaffer saw I was alright he would set me on. This proved to be good advice, and after a few weeks of having a go at all the jobs, and getting as dirty as those who were being paid, I eventually got a job there, attending to tubs of clay being conveyed by an endless rope from the clay hole to the grinding mill, to be made into bricks.

My first week's wage was eight shillings, which went, of course, to Mother for my keep, out of which I received sixpence pocket money – and I was a millionaire! These were high wages for a boy, but the work was very hard and I earned it. However, it didn't last very long, and by the time I reached fifteen I had got a job in the pit at one and sixpence a day, which was about the standard rate. So, for a five and three-quarter day week my wages were eight shillings and seven-pence halfpenny. I went through all the grades of pit work, from operating a hand pump, driving a pony, pushing tubs about, to the actual heaving of the coal.

Pit-work was hard and dangerous. Just getting underground was a perilous operation, and during those early years, I had on many occasions, while waiting at the pit top for the cage to convey us to the pit bottom, wondered what would happen if the winding rope broke. We would all have been dead, of course; workers' safety did not have the same priority attached to it then as it does these days. It was a sobering thought, and it occurred to me on a daily basis that somebody ought to do something about safety – not that I was vain enough to think that I could do anything about it. As the years went on, however, and I had reached the age of eighteen or nineteen, I began to get some ideas about making the pit cage safer, and thought to myself, why not? Why shouldn't I be vain enough to have a go?

At last, after scores of impossible ideas had passed through my mind, an idea struck me which I thought might just work. I turned it over and over in my mind; I would lie awake at night thinking out ways and means of making it work. I decided to try and make a model of it. It was a very crude affair, made from bits and pieces, and I constructed it in the coalhouse at home. The guide ropes, which consisted of part of Mother's clothes line, were secured to the roof and held taut with weights hanging at the bottom. There was a pulley at the top centre over which passed a length of strong string, attached to the bridle chains of the cage so that the cage could be moved up and down, gliding between the guide ropes. I was alone when I made the first tentative trial. It worked. Eureka!

I don't remember where every member of the family was at that wonderful moment; only my mother and father and brother Albert were at home, so I yelled to them to come and have a look. There was not room inside the coalhouse for all of us, so I enlisted Albert as my assistant inside, while Mother and Dad stood at the doorway. I held the end of the string, which acted as the winding rope and moved the cage up and down, and explained how it all worked. Then I fetched a sharp knife from the kitchen and gave it to Albert, explaining to him that while I was moving the cage up and down I wanted him to cut the string without warning. This was a tense moment for me, as I continued moving the cage. Suddenly, it went loose in my hand. Albert had cut the string and there was a slight 'brr' sound, but there was the cage suspended in mid-air.

There was silence for a second or two, then Dad gave an incredulous 'Well, well, well! If that don't beat the band!'

Albert added, 'Marvellous!'

Mother, who was always more worldly wise said quietly and ominously, 'Well done, but don't let it worry you too much.' I suppose she said this because she could see how excited I was and was afraid for me. 'People like us' didn't invent things. However, I felt triumphant, and my moment of triumph was experienced again and again as the other members of my family, friends and relations came for a demonstration. I was in seventh heaven, greatly flattered as different people, friends, and friends of friends came to see it.

This, of course, was a very unethical way to go about things. An invention is supposed to be kept a secret until Letters Patent are obtained. For my ignorance, ethics meant little to me. However, after the first flush of excitement had subsided, I obtained the measurements of the cage at the pit where I worked at the time and constructed, with great difficulty, a scale model – one which could be dissected and carried anywhere for demonstration. It was a splendid model and worked perfectly, and it took over two years to complete.

Albert was my chief mentor in all this, aided and abetted by the rest of the family. The family was beginning to thin out a little now through marriage. Harry, Len and Ernie were all married, which meant that Albert was the only elder brother left at home, and he and I worked hand in glove on this invention.

In 1911 (I was 21) we applied for Letters Patent for my invention – and it passed, and we thought all our troubles were over. We thought that we only had to wait for someone to come along with a ton of

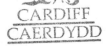

money and we'd be rich, then we could retire and live happily ever after. Such was not the case, however. The following months became very frustrating when no-one got in touch with us.

The manager of the pit where I worked did show a little interest. He expressed a wish to see the model, so we arranged a time and date for me to take it to his office and demonstrate it. He was rather flippant about it as I was assembling it, but when he had seen the first demonstration he seemed very interested and asked many questions about it. In the end he was so enthusiastic that he promised to have a prototype made and tried out at the colliery. This was good news and it lifted our spirits no end. Day after day as I worked at the pit I made enquiries of the blacksmiths and engineers to see if it had been started, but months went by and I concluded that it was not going to be made there.

Then – a bombshell. I had a visitor from London, who had come especially to see my model. He represented the Metropolitan Railway Company – the underground railways. (I must explain here that, in those days, there were no escalators. Passengers were conveyed up and down by means of lifts or hoists.) The Metropolitan Railway Company had sent their representative to examine my safety device for pit cages to see if it could be adapted to their needs. This man's visit was very unexpected and nearly caught me out, for the model had lain idle for quite a long time and I was not sure whether it was going to work.

I need not have worried; it worked beautifully, and the representative was greatly impressed, so much so that he said he was in favour of his company acquiring the patent rights. Such things, he explained, had to be examined and approved by their chief engineer before a final decision could be made. He could not say when the chief engineer would be likely to come, but would let me know. We shook hands and he went away.

The family were all waiting with eagerness to know what had happened, and when I told them all about it they were delighted for me. I was happy too, I thought I was going to be rich, and in this frame of mind I waited, expecting any day to hear that the chief engineer was coming to see me, but as weeks went on without a word, my happiness began to wear a bit thin.

Then, an old workmate of mine at the brickyard came to see me with a request from my old employer, Mr Wilkes, to see the model. I knew that Mr Wilkes could make my device as he also owned a foundry at Pelsall. So, I agreed to take the model for his inspection the following Thursday. I mention the day as it is important.

I duly turned up at his office on the Thursday morning. Mr Wilkes was pleased to see me; he said he remembered me from when I worked at his brickyard. I set up the model ready for working, but Mr Wilkes took control himself and would not let me touch it. I didn't really mind as I knew it would work. To be quite frank, he tried his hardest to crash it, but it stood up to all his endeavours. Then he invited me to sit down and, straight out of the blue said, 'How much do you want for it?'

Taken completely by surprise, I didn't know how to answer him. I was a young, naïve, working class lad, who knew nothing about the workings of business. I heard myself blurt out 'Five hundred pounds' and felt almost ashamed of my own effrontery; to me, five hundred pounds meant five fortunes. To my surprise, he didn't seem at all shocked, and said it was worth it. Then he added that five hundred pounds was a lot of money, and he then asked me what percentage I would like to take if he undertook to manufacture it. I agreed immediately to take fifty per cent.

'Alright,' he replied. 'If you'll let me have a letter to that effect we can get moving.'

I agreed to do that and thought at last that the money was on its way. It made me feel more confident than I had ever felt in my life. Fate, however, was not on my side, and it was not helped by my naïveté and gullibility.

When I got home from that interview, there was a letter waiting for me. It was from the Metropolitan Railway Company to say that the chief engineer, Mr Davies, was coming to see me the next day, Friday. This would have been quite alright except for the fact that I had not got the model; I had left it in Mr Wilkes' office, at his request, and I was now in a quandary. Any other day I could have gone and fetched it back, but Mr Wilkes had gone home and would not be back until Monday morning.

His office was a small, brick-built affair with two small offices about ten feet square, standing alone by the roadside. Only he had the key.

So, what could I do about Mr Davies? This, I have since always considered, was my moment of supreme stupidity. Mother's health was beginning to fail at this time and therefore I did not want to burden her with my problems, and no-one else was at home. There was no-one to advise me and I felt somewhat panicky. I sat down and wrote a letter to Mr Davies and then sent it by Express Letter Post, which would ensure that the letter reached him before he could start his journey the next day.

The content of the letter was roughly as follows:

> Could you please postpone your visit until next Tuesday, as the model of my invention is in the office of Mr Wilkes, who requested a demonstration, and he will not be back in his office until Monday?

I rank that letter as the world's most un-businesslike communication of all time, and there could be only one answer to it. The answer I received was to the effect that sorry, but, they couldn't enter into negotiations while other parties had negotiations in progress. I wrote back immediately to say that the present negotiations were over, but I received no reply.

If I had had my wits about me or at least possessed a little business acumen, I should have told them that the model was out of order, that I had broken something on it, and it would take a few days to repair it, thus gaining time. I slipped up through being honest, and lost the opportunity. 'Honesty is the best policy' might seem a worthy maxim, but a cynic would say, 'Yes, but it keeps you very poor.'

Mr Wilkes at the brickyard? Ah, yes. That gentleman told me, when I went for the model, that he had invented a safety device of his own for the same purpose as mine. He told me that it wasn't exactly like mine, but that he had been inspired by mine to invent something similar, to serve the same purpose.

'What about our agreement?' I asked him.

He replied that *he* had signed nothing. He dismissed me, saying that if anything cropped up he would let me know. I walked out, thoroughly disenchanted. Some time later, I learned that Mr Wilkes had tried his idea out and that it had been a failure. Well, so much for my glittering career as a millionaire inventor!

There is a footnote to this. In 1911, a bill was passed in parliament which, among many other things, compelled mine owners to have their winding ropes changed at certain specific intervals, which meant that the winding ropes would never be allowed to get into a dangerous condition. This was all to the good, and I have never heard of a winding rope breaking since that time. That, I would like to think, is why my invention was never taken up officially.

CHAPTER FOUR

1915 – JOINING KITCHENER'S ARMY

In the last chapter, when I explained about my invention, I jumped a gap of about ten years or so, during which time we had moved house again, twice, first to 50 Church Street, Bloxwich, and then to 60 Church Street. I am not sure if Len got married from number 50, but I know that my elder sister, Edie, did.

There is an episode in Edie's romance that is worth recording, and it illustrates the kind of coarse humour of those days. A young man from Newtown, Tom Walkerdine, was paying court to her, and the road from Newtown to Bloxwich was a very lonely one and was considered to be dangerous to travel along at night, as there was no public transport of any kind. Tom was a big man, about five feet ten and well built, but very shy and diffident. He had well-greased hair and a cultivated roller-curl slanting across his forehead.

He always came to see Edie on a bicycle which he kept in immaculate condition. He would sit on the cross-bar of his bike, one hand on the saddle and the other hand on the handle bars, the bike resting at the kerb, while Edie would be standing at the bottom of the entry all smiles and starched elegance. They would get closer after dark, however.

It seemed ages that it went on like this, and umpteen invitations to come into the house were always bashfully declined. My older brother,

Ernie, who was courting strongly at the time too, got to know him quite well through brushing against them in the entry as he came home. Then, one night, when it was very cold, Mother was concerned about Edie catching cold, and went out herself and at last persuaded him to come in. The best crockery was laid for supper and it was clear that with the welcome we all gave him he was enjoying himself. Then Ernie came home and with a broad grin on his face said to Edie, 'I see you've got im in at last eatin' my supper.'

We all laughed as we knew it was a joke – that is, we all laughed except Tom and Edie. Tom put his knife and fork down and refused to eat any more. We all, especially Ernie, tried to explain it was only a joke but Tom couldn't see it. It was a long time before he came in again, and Tom and Edie resumed their former postures at the bottom of the entry. By familiarity, however, he eventually became as roguish as any of us and would regale us with hair-raising stories of his encounters with vagrants, gangs and the like when returning home late at night.

It was quite common to encounter such people whilst walking or cycling between Bloxwich and neighbouring areas like Newtown and Great Wyrley. The Wyrley Boys, as we called them, used to come in gangs, not necessarily unruly, but on the principle of 'safety in numbers'. The High Street was always thronged on Sunday nights by young men and girls, some standing gossiping and giggling, while others patrolled the street, trying to attract each other's attention, with the hope of pairing up and starting a conversation.

The girls, naturally, knew most of the Bloxwich boys, but the Wyrley boys, being practically foreigners and better dressed than we were, seemed to be preferred by the girls. The girls were mostly servants having their night off; the boys, almost without exception, were miners (job opportunities for the lower classes in the early 1900s were extremely limited for both sexes). I did my share of patrolling Bloxwich High Street on Sunday nights, up until I was about nineteen, when all my spare time was taken up with my invention.

Around this time, 1911 onwards, one or other of us in the family would go and visit our Aunt Ada who lived in Merthyr Tydfil, South

Wales. It was a rare opportunity for a little holiday. Sometimes my sister Gertie would go with me, or my brothers, Albert, Tom or Edgar. Nearly every holiday time some of us would go to Aunt Ada, who was a widow with five children, or they would come to us. It was on one of these visits to Auntie that I met a girl, Agnes, to whom I eventually became engaged. It was a strange kind of courtship as we were only able to see each other three or four times a year; it was mainly a correspondence courtship, and the family, though loath to interfere, were not enthusiastic about it, and really thought I ought to look around for a nice local girl. I shall refer to the outcome of this courtship later on as it lasted until 1917, and I have a lot more to say before then.

The period 1912 to 1914 and 1915 was fraught with many anxieties, chief among them was Mother's failing health. By this time, the family was fairly well off – comparatively speaking – and everyone did their best to get whatever Mother needed to ease her pain. My sister Ada, who was in domestic service in Carters Green, near West Bromwich, was asked to come home and help Mother, which she did. The married members of the family all lived within a mile radius of home, and Harry, Len and Ernie called in on their way home from work every day to see how Mother was. Edie, recently married, lived just across the road, and she too did whatever she could to help out, as did Gertie, who worked at a local factory.

There were no painkilling drugs available to people like us in those days, so what our mother must have suffered can only be imagined. She had cancer of the liver. She was very brave and tried hard to hide the agony she was in, but it was obvious to us all that she was not going to be with us for very much longer. She passed away at the age of only 55 on 12 October 1913. Although her death was not unexpected, it still came as a great shock to us all, but dear old Dad was devastated.

Dad was one of those people who could not cry. It would have been much better for him if he could, and his grief was plain to see, though he fought against it with stoical courage. On the day of the funeral he placed an obligation on us that none of us thought we would be able to carry through. He summoned us all to one room and, in his rough way, pleaded with us to try not to cry at the graveside, 'Cos, if you do,' he said, 'I don't know what I shall do. I shall very likely go mad.' The words may not sound impressive now, but the grief-laden emphasis he placed on them affected everyone, and, though it was almost impossible, we did just manage to stay our tears until we returned home.

It was heart-rending to see Dad like this in bereavement; his world had been moved from its axis and things would never be normal again. Fortunately life goes on, as they say, and it does; not the same, but in a new 'makeshift' kind of way. We settled down eventually to a new routine, Dad becoming 'Chancellor of the Exchequer', and everyone else having to pull their weight. So, we got along quite well. There were five workers to keep the home going: Albert, myself, Gertie, Tom and Edgar. Hilda had just left school and, rather than the usual practice of entering domestic service or getting a job in a factory, she stayed at home to help around the house. Nellie, Frank and George were still in school.

Then another tragedy: in the summer of 1914, Albert had an accident at the pit which put him out of action for a long time. He was injured by a fall of rock. No bones were broken, but his knee was badly damaged and swelled up with fluid to an enormous size. The doctor was in two minds about whether to lance it and let out the fluid, or to give him an injection (of radium, I think it was) 'to disperse it through his body'. The latter method was decided upon and his knee began to shrink back to something like its normal size, and we thought he was getting better. It was not to be, however, for soon afterwards he was laid up with rheumatic fever, and suffered agonies. He could not move a muscle or do a single thing for himself. At times he was delirious, and we began to have sombre forebodings about him.

By this time, the Great War had begun, and I had a burning desire to join the Army, as many of my friends had already done. I wanted so badly to join up; whether it was patriotism or a desire to be 'in the swim', as it were, I cannot say, but I deserved my bottom kicking for thinking of leaving the family in its hour of need. There was Albert – the mainstay of the family – out of action and dangerously ill; then there was me – the next mainstay – desperate to get away. With the wages of Tom, Edgar and Gertie alone it would have been almost impossible to keep the home going. So, I promised Dad that I would not join the Army until Albert was fit for work again. This must have been a great relief to Dad, as it was to the others, but not to me. I wanted to be a 'glory boy' and, looking back on this, I must have been stark-raving mad, and utterly brainwashed by the propaganda being put out.

Britain had a much smaller volunteer army than most other European countries and needed to take concerted measures to encourage young men to sign up. I remember well Lord Kitchener pointing at me personally from innumerable hoardings. He kept telling me that my country needed ME. Then there were girls going around sticking white feathers in young men's lapels, using the slogan 'NO GUN, NO GIRL'. I was not unfortunate enough to receive a white feather; I think that would have been shame more than I could have borne.

It was November 1915, and the war had been raging for over twelve months, when Albert was well enough to work again and I was free to join up, and I did so right away. I was sorry to leave, but my patriotism had not diminished at all over the months, and I was eager to go. I joined the 5th South Staffordshire Regiment after being medically examined with four or five others in an upstairs room over a shop next door to the Red Lion in Park Street, Walsall.

There were two other Bloxwich men, Len Hinks and Bert Lapworth, who enlisted at the same time, along with two men from outside the district. We were all brusquely told to go up the stairs and into the room on the right and get undressed. The room overlooked the back of some houses with an open yard, where women were hanging out washing, and we were somewhat embarrassed to have to undress in front of an un-curtained window. As we hesitantly began to undress, the recruiting sergeant, who had no doubt seen this sort of thing many times before, yelled, 'Come on, gerrum off! Them women down there won't hurt ya!'

When we had 'gorrum off', we had to stand in line in the middle of the room so that the doctor, when he came, could examine us. There was no form of heating in the room and it was freezing cold, and the doctor was in no hurry to attend to us. I'll say this for him, when the doctor finally did make an appearance, he had the coldest stethoscope in the world. On the way out we had to sign our names, after which we each received a shilling – the King's Shilling. Now we were in the Army. We were told to report to Walsall railway station the following morning.

As I walked back down the stairs, I realised that the over-inflated balloon of enthusiasm I had nursed for so long had sustained a slow puncture. This wasn't because I felt any less committed, but because of the complete lack of anything resembling courtesy by the recruiting staff. None of us expected to be patted on the back exactly, but then neither did we expect to be bawled at as we were, or left standing about in our birthday suits until the doctor felt inclined to honour us with his presence. This little episode was our first taste of 'things to come'; it was our first lesson in army discipline and it was mild in comparison to others that followed.

Next day, we arrived at Whittington Barracks in Lichfield, where we were fitted out with uniform and kit, and where, over the next week, we received our preliminary training in basic drills. Then we were sent on to Rugeley Camp, on Cannock Chase, for our real training. Rugeley Camp covered a huge area, and there were many thousands of soldiers training there, representing most units of the Army.

At first our training was confined to drilling and marching. The accent seemed to be on attaining physical fitness, which was fine by me. I was as fit as a fiddle and had been doing physical jerks for years on the horizontal bar and the hanging rings, so that part of the training was enjoyable to me. After the first week at Rugeley, we were pleasantly surprised to learn that there were no weekend parades and that those who lived within a reasonable distance could go home on Saturday mornings and return on Sunday nights. So, I was able to go home every weekend for the next few weeks.

Then one weekend, as I was looking forward to going home as usual, we heard that orders had been issued to all units that we were to be confined to barracks; our weekend leave was cancelled. There was no reason given for the order, but we soon learned from the staff that this was the usual practice when a draft was about to leave for the battle-front. It was too late for us all to write home to say we couldn't leave, so we just had to stay put; there was nothing we could do about it. We were all rather gloomy as we sat around the stove on the Saturday morning, desperate to get away from camp for a bit – and then one of the boys came up with an idea.

The idea was for a group of us to leave camp, but, instead of walking out in twos and threes, higgledy-piggledy and bound to get noticed, we should march out in formation as though we were a working party off to do a job; in other words a 'fatigue party' to use the Army expression. This sounded like a great idea, except who was going to lead the party? We had no NCOs, but we were fortunate in having in the hut an old soldier who knew the Army law in such a case. He explained to us that in the absence of an officer or NCO, the longest-serving soldier takes charge. So then the question was: who was the longest-serving soldier amongst our group? The answer was that we had all enlisted on the same day – deadlock!

Then it came down to what *time* we had enlisted, and we discovered that Garnet Davies had enlisted about an hour before the rest of us. He declined to lead. Deadlock again! So, we decided to draw lots for it. And guess who won? Yes, me. I really wasn't keen, but I accepted it. We formed up outside in two ranks, four in each rank. I told them before we started off to remember to act as if it was real, and if all went well we would be out of the camp in ten minutes.

The operation went beautifully, and as we passed the armed sentries, at intervals I gave the order 'eyes right' or 'eyes left', and I saluted each sentry and got his return salute. 'Eyes front' after passing the last sentry was exhilarating and I could see that the boys were inclined to break up, but I knew that we could still be seen from the camp and reminded them to keep it up until we were out of sight. Then it was every man for himself. We did not go into Hednesford to get a bus, as was usual, in case there were military police there; instead, we set off on foot to Cannock.

When we got to Cannock, we felt we would appreciate a ride some-where after the long walk, so we waited for a bus. When it came there were several officers on board and our guilty consciences warned us that it was too risky to get on. So, we kept on walking until we got to Bloxwich. This was a good walk, the distance from Rugeley to Bloxwich via Cannock being something in the region of ten miles. My two Bloxwich friends and I were home, the rest of them went to the railway station to travel on to Dudley, West Bromwich, Brierly Hill and the Lye.

We returned on Sunday night as usual. We had been rumbled, of course. It was hardly surprising considering there were about 40 men in the hut. There is always someone ready to put the dampers on enterprise. It transpired that we were summoned to appear before the commanding officer on the Monday morning, and he gave us a stern lecture about the seriousness of our action, our irresponsibility, our lack of discipline, and goodness knows what. He ended up by fining us three days' pay. Our pay, being a shilling a day, was reduced from seven shillings to four for that week – but we thought it had been worth it.

I don't remember clearly exactly how long I was at Rugeley Camp, but I was certainly there long enough to learn how to handle a rifle in arms drill, how to take aim and fire the rifle at the butts. We took part in exercises and manoeuvres amongst the hills around Rugeley and Brocton. Then an order came through to send a certain number of men to Harrowby Camp in Grantham for training on the Vickers light automatic machine gun. I was hoping I would not be one of them as it would put a stop to my weekends at home, but when the names were called out, mine was among them, and, strangely enough, so were the names of my two Bloxwich pals, Len Hinks and Bert Lapworth, and four others from the little escapade I have just described. It seemed a strange coincidence that out of a company of 100–150 men we should be chosen – but there it was.

So, off we went to Grantham. And what a dump it was! We were met by a Scottish sergeant from the Black Watch whose name was Lumsden. He seemed a nice chap and easy to talk to. He was our Hut-Sergeant, and we were the first batch to arrive. He did his best to explain to us what it was all about. There was little activity or organisation at this stage, with only a skeleton staff until the arrival of the rest of the units from all parts of Britain. I remember it was raining and the place was a quagmire, and we were very hungry. We spoke to Sergeant Lumsden and he managed to get us a bit of food from the cookhouse. There was only one cook until the camp filled up, and we had to buy food from a café just outside the camp gates until proper facilities could be set up.

When the rest of the units had arrived we were gathered together and told why we had been brought there. It seemed that, up to that point, each infantry battalion had been using their heavy Vickers machine guns as each individual company commander had seen fit. Each battalion had two Vickers guns each, I believe, but to get the best from these guns they needed specially trained men and tactics, so, in many cases, the fire-power of the Vickers gun was being neglected and its value lost. The High Command had therefore decided that the Vickers guns should be withdrawn from use in the infantry and replaced by the Lewis machine gun, which was more mobile and could be carried by one man, and that a specialist corps of men should be formed to operate the Vickers guns. And so it was that men with mechanical ability and initiative were chosen from all regiments across the British Army and brought together to be trained exclusively in the use of the Vickers gun. Our egos were boosted to think we had been specifically chosen for this task. We were to be known as the Machine Gun Corps, our Company to be known as the 71st Company.

It was interesting to note the many different cap badges, and we must have looked a motley mob when on parade, as compared to a regimental company all wearing the same kind of cap badge. However, we were anything but a motley mob once our machine gun training got underway, and in due course we were issued with our new cap badges: two crossed Vickers guns surmounted by the royal crown. The new badge, from a distance, looked not unlike the skull and crossbones.

The following two months were occupied with very intensive training. We learned the little text book by heart from cover to cover until each machine part was as familiar as our own fingernails. We all became so adept at handling the machine gun that any one of us could reassemble it in less than a minute from all the bits and pieces in a heap. We also had to master map reading and learn to take compass bearings.

Throughout this time there was, naturally, much speculation about when we would be putting our new-found skills into action – and where. We were soon to find out.

CHAPTER FIVE

DEPARTURE FOR THE WESTERN FRONT

It was March 1916 when we had our first leave from Grantham. It proved to be our pre-embarkation leave. I had been in the Army for less than four months.

We did not know for certain when or where we would be sent, but we had a good notion that something was cooking – and the 'bush telegraph' was seldom wrong. There were rumours that our Company was going to Salonika, some said it was going to be Mesopotamia. The destination, however, turned out to be France. We were going to the Western Front. Just our luck!

We spent an afternoon loading a special train with guns, limbers (the detachable front part of the gun carriage) and mules in preparation for our night departure. We were marched to the railway station in the late evening and boarded the train, and, to our surprise and delight, there was a large crowd waiting to see us off. We had not expected this; on our frequent incursions to Grantham we had found the people aloof to say the least. I suppose in a military town the people become understandably sick and tired of seeing soldiers; nevertheless, it was obviously a tradition to give a send-off to any unit bound for the Front. As the train pulled out, the crowd cheered and I heard people shout 'Good luck!' and 'Come back soon!', 'Keep your peckers up!' and so on, while we, for our part, were at the carriage windows waving like maniacs. When we were away from the station lights, we settled down for our journey to Southampton.

It was blowing a gale in Southampton. Great waves were lashing the quayside where the little steamer, which was waiting to take us across the Channel, was moored, and it was bobbing up and down like a yo-yo. The plan was that we were to go aboard immediately and set sail that morning, but the captain of the vessel said that it was not advisable to attempt a crossing until the storm had abated. Our departure was postponed until the afternoon, but the afternoon was no better, nor the evening. It was late into the night before the gales subsided a little and we were allowed to go aboard, by which time we were all fed up to the eyebrows and stiff with cold through waiting about all day in the storm.

The vessel was a paddle-steamer, used in peacetime for cross-channel summer trips. It was hardly suitable for making the crossing in such weather and we were apprehensive to say the least. We never knew the name of the vessel, but I think it must have been the original *Skylark* for it tossed up and down, forwards and sideways, and threatened to founder at any minute. Even the crew were seasick. The captain, we heard later, lost contact with our escorting destroyers, which then spotted us but couldn't identify us. They signalled to ask who we were, then threatened to fire on us if we didn't answer. Miraculously, someone managed to get an answer to them just in time! Thankfully, we knew nothing of this at the time. However, considering the condition we were in, we probably wouldn't have cared much, for we were all in a sorry state. The sea was far too rough for us to even lean over the rail to be sick, so many of us spent the voyage gripping the lower rail with one hand whilst lying flat with our faces in the gutters.

We laughed about it later, but at the time, my first experience of *mal de mer* was no laughing matter. I have crossed the Channel several times since that night, but never a crossing like that one, thank goodness.

We arrived at Le Havre just before daybreak and went ashore, immensely relieved to be on dry land once more. There seemed to be no hurry to continue on our way, as I daresay the officers felt no more like marching than we did. We were all physically fit men, though, and it did not take long to recover from our experience, and about 9am we were marched off up the cobbled streets of the town. My impression was that it didn't seem a particularly bright sort of place, but there were plenty of kids following us, chanting 'Souvenir! Souvenir!' and some other French phrases, the meaning of which we had not the faintest idea.

I was marching alongside Garnet Davies (from the Lye, near Stourbridge). He had a dry, Black Country sense of humour, and after we had been listening to the kids and trying to understand what they were saying, he remarked, 'Ain't it funny? Even the kids here can talk French.'

We were soon out of Le Havre and came to a camp on the outskirts of the town, where the field kitchens were busy cooking breakfast. The smell was tantalising. Our seasickness quite gone, we were ready for something to eat.

Over the next few days and nights we moved north, by train and then a series of long marches and stops, during which time we slept in all kinds of places – barns, old houses and sheds – anywhere where there was some kind of roof over us, until we reached a camp just outside Poperinghe, in Belgium. It was there that we were told to wait for our orders, which gave us time to get de-loused (on the long journey from the coast, every man jack had become as lousy as it is possible to get – a condition we had to live with throughout the war). My first inkling of this was when I saw some of the lads with their shirts off at night and examining them. I had felt nothing, but I thought I should have a look myself anyway. I was so disgusted when I discovered I had lice that I took off all my underclothes and threw them away, not caring what the Army or anyone else might say about it. It was a rash thing to do in the middle of March, but actually I didn't catch so much as a sniffle.

We had been in the camp for several days when we learned of a Durham man, I think his name was Benson, who was boasting that he was the champion boxer of the Company, and the officers, who no doubt sensed a little diversion from routine, offered five francs to anyone who would, or could, stand three rounds with this man. All the Company was present, and the Company Sergeant Major was walking around with his notebook, looking for someone to volunteer.

Our little group, Davies, Hinks, Lapworth and myself, were standing together and were surprised when Davies suddenly piped up, 'I think I'll 'ave a go at 'im.' We tried our best to dissuade him, but in his off-hand way he said, 'We've got no money, 'ave we?'

'No,' we said, 'but we don't want you to get knocked about just for that.'

But the CSM was now close to us and Davies told him to put his name down. We felt a bit sorry for Davies to have to take on this man just to get a few francs to spend on us, and even more so when Benson himself came up to us and advised Davies not to go on with it as he was afraid of hurting him. 'You see,' he said, 'they call me "the Tiger", and when I get going I don't know me own strength.' But Davies was adamant he needed the money and would go on.

An impromptu ring was rigged up and the contestants introduced. Then, with the CO acting as referee, the match began. Davies was the taller of the two men, but Benson had unusually long arms and a thick-set body, and looked a formidable opponent.

They circled around each other for a bit, then Benson tried to land a right hook, but Davies dodged it quite easily; in fact, as time went on, he conducted himself with increasing confidence. Benson seemed surprised, but not as surprised as we were that Davies had been holding out on us, for it soon became obvious that this was not the first time our pal had been in a boxing ring. Davies tried an uppercut, which, if it had caught his opponent would surely have lifted him clean off the ground; it missed only by a whisker, but that was close enough for Benson apparently, who fell to the ground as though in agony, shouting, 'I never thought you'd do a thing like that, Garnet!' He was inferring, of course, that he had been hit below the belt (despite the fact the neither boxer had managed to lay a glove on the other), a tactic obviously designed to bail himself out of the ring before Davies could really hurt him. Davies was embarrassed and protested to the referee that he hadn't touched Benson. The referee assured him that he had seen it all, and awarded Davies the five francs.

We spent the money that evening. There were still a few civilians in the area and we could find places where we could buy beer at a penny a glass. The beer was poor stuff, but being able to sit down and talk to people who were not in uniform was compensation enough. During the evening we discovered that Davies had, in fact, been a local boxing champion in the Lye and Stourbridge area – which just goes to show you never know who you are talking to when everyone is in uniform.

Davies' victory brought out a facet of human nature which is more common than generally thought; it was illustrated by the actions of the CSM. Up until that time, the CSM seemed to have a down on us Midlanders. He wasn't vicious, but he was forever niggling and finding fault with us, especially on drill parades, when the slightest error would bring down his censures upon us. Not that we were any worse than the others; we wondered at times if it was our thick Midlands dialect he didn't like, but whatever it was, after the boxing match, the CSM's attitude towards us completely changed. He didn't exactly grant us any extra favours, but he at least treated us in the same way as the others. And we suddenly found that life in the Army was a little easier for us.

A few days after this, we received our orders to go 'up the line.' We were going to the Ypres Salient. Thus came the moment of truth – the moment we had been trained for. Only half our Company was to go up to the trenches on that occasion, and I was among them. I won't attempt to describe the feelings of my pals and those around me when the order came, only my own, although I suspect their feelings were similar to mine. I would not say I was *frightened* exactly, but I had a feeling in my stomach that was not comfortable or reassuring. I think it was more a fear of the unknown, and the realisation that I was at last to come face to face with the enemy. However, my Rowbotham optimism came to my rescue in that moment (the Rowbothams have always been an optimistic lot). I thought to myself, Look, thousands of others have gone through wars before you and come out alright, so why shouldn't you? The Rowbotham optimism was, of course, ignoring the small matter of the thousands of others before me who had not come out alright. Looking back, I also recall a sense of fatalism: 'What is to be will be' or, to put it the soldiers' way, 'If your name isn't on it, you won't get it.'

So, we were formed up just before dusk and marched off. The conversations among the men were cheerful enough, some even cracked the odd joke. It was like whistling in the dark. After we had been marching a mile or two, a stray dog joined us and followed us for some time, sniffing at one and then another, until he had inspected the lot of us, and then, not finding whatever or whoever he was looking for, turned back. We thought what a lucky dog he was to be going in the opposite direction.

We were nearing the trenches, and before entering the communications trench we were told that from then on there must be no talking. It was vital to make as little noise as possible or we might be shelled. So, on we went, not daring to speak above a whisper, until we were brought to a halt. Then, our section was divided up: two out of the four gun teams were marched off to the right, one team to the left, and the last, ours, was marched straight ahead, onto the front line.

Our gun team comprised six men and a corporal, plus a gun, tripod, boxes of filled belts of ammunition, rations and equipment. We were surprised at what we saw as we entered the front line of trenches. The sentries and the other men all had on their gas masks, and in the semi darkness they looked like something out of a science fiction book. There was a gas alert on, and the wind was blowing towards our trenches from the German side, but no-one had thought to tell us! We might easily have been gassed if the Jerries had made a gas attack. Poisonous chlorine gas had been used as a weapon by the Germans for some months by then. It left any unprotected soldiers on the front line choking and blinded (the gas formed into a sort of foaming liquid in a man's lungs and 'drowned him' – a terrifying way to die). Fortunately for us that night, the Jerries didn't make a gas attack. We had gas masks, of course, but if we had walked into it, we would have had no time to put them on.

Our gas masks in 1916 were of the earliest type, rendering the wearer practically blind through misting-up. The mask itself was made of a thick kind of flannel, impregnated with a chemical which made it a grey-green colour, and was in the shape of a shoulder-length hood. The hood had goggles and a mouthpiece through which you could only breathe outwards. The inward breathing had to be done through the nose, with the air filtered through the material of the hood. It was difficult to put on; first the tunic had to be unbuttoned and folded back over the shoulders, then the hood pulled over the head and the mouthpiece inserted into the mouth, the goggles lined up with the eyes, the lower part of the hood placed round the shoulders and the tunic then buttoned up again. This sounds a lengthy operation, but we had had much previous practice and could do it in seconds. Once it was on, you had a feeling of isolation from your fellow men, not being able to talk or see very well through the thick fog of mist on the goggles. Fortunately, a better designed gas mask was introduced later on which had an anti-mist preparation.

So, we were in the trenches at last! We set to mounting the gun in the emplacement and then training it onto German lines. Then, the Corporal posted two sentries in the emplacement while the other four men 'rested' in a small ramshackle dugout a few yards behind. The sentries were relieved every two hours, which meant that we would be on sentry for two hours and 'off' for four hours. All conversations were carried on in stage-whispers, as we were told that the Germans were close enough to hear ordinary speech.

This was a 'quiet' front, comparatively speaking, and there was not much heavy firing going on – just a shell or two and the distant chatter of machine guns and rifle fire. It didn't seem so bad after all.

Later that night, however, we had a very rude awakening. My mate and I had just come off sentry duty and were sitting in the dugout, when there was a terrific explosion, not more than two or three yards behind our dugout. It dislodged some of the dugout's supports, and we were lucky it didn't collapse. A slightly shorter range of the German gun would have seen us off this mortal coil in less than five hours serving on the front line! We were unhurt – but it hadn't done much for our nerves. Still, I thought, the old Rowbotham optimism surfacing briefly, a miss was as good as a mile, wasn't it?

The remainder of my first night in the trenches was quiet, thankfully, and just before dawn came, the whispered order along the trench was 'stand to', which meant that all ranks and units should be alert and prepared to meet an attack from the enemy – an apprehensive time. The attack didn't come however, and by full daylight we received the order to 'stand down'. After 'stand down', the Corporal posted one sentry only, his duty being to keep a sharp look-out for enemy movement and to report anything unusual, or, if an attack was to come, to fire the gun, which would bring us all out.

The biggest shock that came with full daylight was the discovery that our gun team was not, in fact, on the front line at all, but ahead of it. We had actually been sent out into no-man's-land. No wonder we had to be quiet!

We had brought sufficient rations with us to last 24 hours, so we had enough food until further supplies could be brought to us after dark. We passed the day sleeping, eating and taking turns on sentry duty. There was some shelling on both sides during the day, but none came as close to us as the one in the night that nearly ended our army careers. The first day in the trenches seemed to pass extremely slowly. It became rather boring in fact (all soldiers will tell you that life in the trenches was a strange mixture of total boredom and utter terror), especially as we could not talk normally.

The day came to an end at last, and the whispered order came down the line again to 'stand to'. We took up our positions in readiness for a possible German attack which happily did not come, and so, after the 'stand down' came, we prepared to carry on the same routine as the night before. Then we had a pleasant surprise. We thought at first that it was our ration party arriving, but it turned out to be our relief party. It seemed that the infantry division we were fighting alongside had been in the trenches for some considerable time and was being relieved, and as our machine gun company was now attached to it, we were being relieved also. We had now become part of the Sixth Infantry Division, and apparently, we were due for a month's 'rest' —I wasn't going to complain.

However, the word 'rest', we discovered, was something of a misnomer, for it consisted of some really hard work and intensive re-training. From the British Army's point of view, the need to re-train was understandable: when men have been living a mole-like existence with no exercise and few facilities for three or four months on end, they tended to become lethargic and out of condition. So, the Sixth Infantry Division was relieved for re-training after a long spell in the trenches, and we went with them, after our short one.

We didn't go back to Poperinghe. Next day, we were on the march once again, to a large camp not far from Calais, where we did a further month's training in tactics and field exercises in conjunction with divisional troops. We also had pep talks from various officers, who all had their own pet theory as to how to induce men to give of their best. One such officer, in particular, gave us his theories in a long discourse on *esprit de corps*. He started by saying that he didn't suppose we knew what it meant. He was damned right — we didn't. He went on to tell us that every man should strive to become the best soldier in his platoon, and that his platoon should be the best in the company, and the company should be the best in the battalion, the brigade, the division, and finally, the best army in the world — making each soldier the best soldier in the world. I suppose the lecture must have had some effect on us, except we didn't so much want to be the most proficient soldiers in the world as the most alive and uninjured!

About the end of April 1916, our 'rest' was over and we set off, foot-slogging it all the way back to the line. Our line was the Ypres Salient, that great semi-circular line which was so notorious in 1914 and 1915 for the First and Second Battles of Ypres. Ypres was one of the cities where the great German push for Paris was halted. Ypres was in ruins, a desolate place, and the skyline at night looked to me like a massive row of broken bottles on a wall, a sinister silhouette of death and destruction.

It was in the salient that we had our first casualty – Bert Lapworth. We were in the trenches in open country and, after a fairly quiet night, the enemy began shelling our positions from early in the morning. One of the very last of their shells that morning to explode anywhere near to us caused a piece of shrapnel to fly up and it struck Bert on the side of his steel helmet. We heard the 'ping' on his helmet, saw him reel against the side of the trench, and rushed to him to see how bad it was. The shrapnel had made a huge dent in his helmet and Bert was dazed, but he soon came round, and as there was no wound, we thought it was a lucky one. He joked about it at the time which created some relieved laughter. His helmet didn't fit him anymore due to the bulge inside it, which made it rock like a see-saw on his head.

Later in the day, however, he began to act strangely, his speech became odd and he started talking gibberish. Although he continued to have some lucid moments, it was plain to see that he was not well, and the Corporal decided to send him back to headquarters when the ration party came in that evening. He was sent straight on to the field hospital and from there back home to England. He had severe concussion and would certainly not be returning to the front again.

We thought how lucky he was to get a 'Blighty One' so soon. Everyone's hope was to get a 'Blighty One' – an injury not too severe, but enough to get us sent back to England, hence the saying 'Lucky Blighter'. How quickly our surge of patriotism and eagerness to fight for our country had dissipated! After only a few months on the front line all we wanted was to be back in England, which seemed so far away. In such a short time we had become completely disillusioned with war, and not just because we had to fight and take life whilst risking our own lives, but because the front line soldier was the most neglected and ill-treated of all men. Even the supplies that came through to us had all been ransacked, except for ammunition and gun spares. The men at base would give all the food supplies the once-over and help themselves to anything they fancied; there was good money to be made flogging food to civilians. Then the divisional base would take their pick, then the brigade, the battalion, and finally company HQ. Once the officers' mess was catered for, whatever was left – not much by that time – was then rationed out for us. I would probably have done the same myself, given the chance, but at the time, when we sometimes would not see a loaf of bread for weeks, it was not quite so easy to see their viewpoint.

Two things, though, we were rarely short of: bully beef and biscuits. Now, whilst being quite sufficient to sustain us and keep us alive, they were hardly appetising fare. Those biscuits were like slabs of concrete. They measured about four inches by three, and about three quarters of an inch thick – and would probably have made a very good floor tile. They were very hard (slight understatement) and would take a long time to eat, but very nourishing. Necessity, as the saying goes, is the mother of invention, and a method of softening them was soon discovered. Our mess tins were just about big enough to take four of these biscuits, and if we soaked them in water for a minute of so to cover them, then in about three hours they would have swelled up to more than twice their size to completely fill the mess tin. These could then be eaten more easily and our hunger satisfied more quickly – and they didn't break your teeth in the process.

I don't want to give the impression that we did not get enough to eat; our grouse was not that we went hungry, but that our diet was so lacking in variety. It was bully beef, bully beef or bully beef. Our only chance of having something different to eat was when we were out of the trenches and at our forward HQ, where we would eat stews of fresh meat and vegetables, and have the occasional treat of suet pudding for afters.

Bread was our most urgent requirement. We were lucky if we got one slice of bread, which we would hoard until teatime and spread with butter and plum and apple jam, if we had some. Plum and apple jam seemed to be the only variety of jam available for some reason. Towards the end of the war it was a delight to see other kinds of jam appearing in the supplies.

Our staple protein, as I mentioned, was the ubiquitous bully beef (corned beef), and some varieties were nicer than others. My favourite was Fray Bentos; it contained quite a bit more fat than other brands and had a meatier taste than some of the other stuff we were given. Later, another type of tinned food reached us. It was known as 'Machonachie Ration' and it contained enough meat and vegetables for one man, supposedly. It looked good, but was always disappointing as it had a peculiar tang which seemed to take away most of the flavour. The food was satisfying but tasted pretty grim.

I want to try and describe something of what life was like around the Ypres Salient ('Wipers', as we called it) during the first three or four months of our stay there. We had become familiar with the names of places around us, like Hill 60, Vimy Ridge, Lens, Menin Gate, Zillebeke, Zonnebeke, Hellfire Corner, and many others. So many incidents occurred during these months that I hardly know where to begin. Let me say first of all that we did not make any attacks on the German lines, nor did they attack us: that is to say, we did not go 'over the top', but both sides were subjected to severe poundings by shell-fire, mortar-fire and 'whizz-bangs'. A 'whizz-bang' was a very high velocity shell which exploded in the air above the trenches, and the velocity was such that it could catch us by surprise, and often did. The missile we dreaded most however was the *minenwerfer*, a large mortar shell which, when it hit the ground, would explode with a terrifying force. At night-time it could not be seen coming, but in the day whoever happened to be on sentry duty would keep his ears cocked for a loud 'plop' from the German lines, then he would scan the sky and be able to see the *minenwerfer* rolling over and over in its trajectory, and alert us to take cover.

I remember one very sad incident concerning a *minenwerfer*, or 'minnie', as we called them. I am not going to give the man's name because if ever a relative of the man were to read this it would cause distress in consequence of what followed. We had received some new men, reinforcements to replace men we had lost during some of the heavy bombardments we had been subjected to. I had been made up to lance corporal by this time and I was in charge of the gun team. The gun position we were in had an underground dugout. It was not a deep dugout – there was only about four or five feet of earth above us. As we had been expecting a German raid we had all been at 'stand to' all night. So, when 'stand down' came I posted a single sentry as usual. The man was one of the newcomers, a smart chap who knew his job as a machine gunner, but it was his first time in the trenches, so I stayed with him a little while as the Germans were sending the occasional minnie. Several came over while I was with him and had listened with him to the tell-tale 'plop' and told him to watch which way the minnie was coming and, if it was heading our way, to dive down sharpish into the dugout. He forgot my advice. He must have been standing in the doorway of the dugout with his back towards us – and his back to the Germans. Suddenly there was a terrific explosion and the poor chap came tumbling backwards down the steps. He was dead, killed instantly by the blast of the explosion; the mortar had not hit our position, it must have been at least a dozen yards away, but the blast had been enough to kill him. We were all a bit gloomy for the rest of the day, as we could not move him until nightfall when we could send for the stretcher-bearers.

Moments like that were very distressing to the other men immediately concerned, but we had no other option but to get on with it. With sudden death threatening any or all of us at any moment we just had to close our mind to everything except the job in hand. It was pointless to dwell on death or the futility and stupidity of war.

When nightfall came I sent for the stretcher-bearers to take him to the rear of the fighting where he could be decently buried, but the stretcher-bearers couldn't come as they were busy with other casualties in nearby units. However, they did send a stretcher and I had to send two of my own men to take the body. There was a tremendous amount of shelling going on which seemed to be concentrated on the communications trenches. It was the hour when rations and supplies were coming up and the Jerries always gave the lines of communication a bashing at this time. It seemed that my two men with their grim burden could not make proper progress down the trenches through meeting parties of men coming in the opposite direction, so they must have decided to get out of the trench and walk along the top. The heaped-up spoil from the trench made a very unstable footpath. Outside the trench the soil was a morass through the continual scooping of water and mud from the trench, and also the incessant rainy weather we had been having. Eventually the men came back saying what a terrible time they'd had getting the body to the makeshift mortuary.

Two days later it was our turn to be relieved and so we went back to forward HQ where I collected the unfortunate man's effects and sent them home with a letter to his mother who, in reply, apart from expressing her grief, asked me to write again telling her where her son was buried so that she could visit the grave after the war. Names of places or information on the whereabouts of military units or personnel were strictly forbidden in letters home, so I told her this in my reply and suggested I call on her when I had a home furlough. This satisfied her and she said she would be very pleased to see me. During this correspondence we had been in the trenches and back out again, and to get the information about where our comrade was buried I had made enquiries at the cemetery and searched the register but I could not find the name I was looking for. I even searched among the newest graves in case of an error, but could find no trace of him. I then went to another cemetery about five miles away as it was just possible his body might have been taken there, but they had no record of him either.

So, what happened to him? I could only conclude that the two men who carried him away must have slipped on the uneven and slimy surface on top of the trench and fallen into the morass below and that the body had fallen off the stretcher into the mud, making it impossible to recover. I couldn't blame the men as they were not only struggling against the terrible conditions underfoot but were being subjected to heavy enemy fire at the same time. Whether this is what happened I never knew for sure, but I knew that I could not write and tell this lad's mother that her son did not have a proper grave. So, I dropped the correspondence, letting her believe that I too had suffered the same fate – may God forgive me. And the lad? He became one of the many thousands of bodies never properly buried, never identified.

By this time, I suppose you could say that we had become 'seasoned warriors', hardened and fatalistic, both qualities being necessary for retaining a reasonable level of sanity in the conditions in which we lived and fought. It was not quite all mud and blood, however. Believe it or not, we had some good times, such as when we received our letters and parcels from home, or when we got out of the trenches for a few days and could enjoy a drink at an estaminet (café) and some contact with civilians, this latter being the most pleasurable as it reminded us of home. We had much admiration for the civilians, making a precarious living only a few miles from the front line. They had also become a little hardened and fatalistic as they often had casualties too, and when we commiserated with them they would answer resignedly, '*c'est la guerre.*'

The casualties continued to be high, and trench-life continued to be wet and muddy and bleak. I recall another story from the Ypres Salient during the first few months of 1916. It concerned my pal Garnet Davies, the boxer; by the time of this incident we had become like brothers to each other, as we were the only two Midlanders remaining of the original nine, the others having been either killed or badly wounded and out of action. Garnet Davies was a young married man at the start of the war, and his wife had recently given birth to their first baby, a son.

We were occupying a secret gun position, selected for us to cover any sudden attack by the Germans on our sparsely manned front line. We knew that if an attack was coming it would come either at dawn or dusk; therefore, to keep our gun position secret, the gun would be mounted at dusk and then manned all night by the whole gun team. At dawn we would dismount the gun and retreat about 100 yards to a dugout, where one man would be posted as sentry, each man taking his turn while the others slept or ate. Sleeping usually occupied the first few hours after breakfast, and on this particular day we had been asleep for some time when Davies woke me up with 'I shall have to have a doctor, Ted.'

Thinking this was one of his daft jokes, I said, 'Go back to sleep, you big mutt.' Expecting Davies to reply, when he did not I sat up and looked over at him. I don't think he knew where he was, and he was shaking and shivering as though he was hooked up to a massage machine – yet it was quite warm inside the dugout. I realised then there was something wrong. I said, 'What's up mate?'

'I'm as cold as a bloody Eskimo,' he replied.

His face was grey and by now I was frightened for him. I knew I had to do something for him, but wasn't really sure what might help. I tried to warm him up; I rolled him over and got a pair of socks and, with one sock on each hand, rubbed him briskly all over, until he cried out to me, 'For God's sake, stop it, mate. You're rubbing holes in me!' It stopped his shivering though. Then I made him comfortable and took some blankets off the other men (they stopped being indignant when they discovered why and were only too glad to help) and covered him up and he went to sleep for a while.

The day seemed endless with poor old Davies in this condition and needing medical attention badly. We were almost certain he had contracted trench fever. Trench fever was a disease a bit like flu, with a high temperature and aches, and it could put men out of action for weeks. It was caused by our infestations of body lice, so not uncommon in the filthy conditions in which we were living. During the day Davies had a few short spells of sleep from which he awoke uttering gibberish, then he had moments of lucidity, and so it was until dusk when the ration party came with the supplies. There was a stretcher in the dugout and we put him on it, and asked the ration party to take him with them. As we were making him comfortable he reached for my hand and asked me to write to his wife, then he lapsed into unconsciousness.

I learned later that he was unconscious for three days, and when I saw him again about two months later he was but a shadow of his former self, and looked very pale and haggard. I saw him because he had left his hospital bed and 'escaped' when he had heard that our Company had been brought back from the line for a short rest. As it happened we were billeted in a barn about a mile or so from the hospital where Davies was a patient. We had no idea of this of course, and were surprised to see a figure, not too steady on his feet, coming up the road. As he got nearer I thought to myself, 'That looks like Garn Davies,' and sure enough it was. He was nearly on the point of collapse, so three of us took hold of him and helped him to the billet and laid him on the straw. We made him comfortable and after a while he told us his story.

He had been taken out of the trenches to a monastery which was being used as a hospital and staffed by the resident Sisters of Mercy. His bed was close to the altar on which there were candles burning, and as he slowly regained consciousness he thought he was dead and in heaven! A Sister of Mercy was gazing down at him and he asked her if she was an angel. She had smiled at him and told him he wasn't dead, but he had been very sick and was now on the mend. It had been touch and go with him – trench fever cost the lives of many men – but Davies eventually became well enough to return to his unit.

CHAPTER SIX

YPRES – LIFE UNDER FIRE

Our Machine Gun Company operated in the Ypres Salient from March 1916 to around August of the same year. It was on 1 July 1916 that the Somme offensive began with the most appalling loss of life – nearly 60,000 British soldiers dead or wounded on the first day. Our troops there were on the offensive, with varying degrees of intensity, up to the end of 1917. The part that our Division (the 6th) took in that offensive I will come to later. Meanwhile, I will try to describe some of the incidents that stand out in my mind which took place while we were still in the Ypres Salient.

I want to say something about our officer, 2nd Lieutenant Van Someren. When he first joined us we were a bit suspicious of him because, in our ignorance, we thought his name was German, not realising that it was in fact Dutch. He was a quiet, soft-spoken man, quite unassuming, but what he didn't know about machine gunnery wasn't worth mentioning. He was our section officer, which meant he was in command of four machine guns and about 30 NCOs and men. He also had a good sense of humour. I remember an instance when we were temporarily in reserve and the order of the day was gun-cleaning, belt-filling, and generally overhauling everything in readiness for the next spell in the trenches. I was still a lance corporal and in charge of one of the gun teams. We had practically done all the work that needed doing, and one of the men, Private Pickering, was standing with his hands in his pockets (usually referred to as 'having your Nottingham gloves on'). Pickering had no idea that Van Someren was approaching from behind. I saw him coming but had no time to warn Pickering without being overheard by the officer. In fact, my own status as the 'man in charge' could be criticised for allowing a man to stand around with his hands in his pockets, so I had to think quickly, for I could sense Van Someren was watching to see what I would do. As though I had only just noticed Pickering with his hands in his pockets, I called out to him, 'Pickering! You'll catch your death o' cold standing there with your Nottingham gloves on!'

The very fact of calling him Pickering – it was always 'Pick' except on parade – was enough for him to realise there was something up; he guessed there was an officer nearby. He hastily withdrew his hands from his pockets and pretended to be working. The effect on Van Someren, however, was not what I expected. Most officers would have called me aside and given me a stern reprimand and a long lecture on army discipline, but instead Van Someren's eyes twinkled, and I could see he was having difficulty suppressing a laugh as he turned away from us. We all agreed he was a decent bloke – which indeed he turned out to be.

On another occasion we were on what was called an observation march. On such a march we were supposed to take in and remember all that we saw – like human cameras – and were then questioned on our return. It is surprising how little registers in the mind in the ordinary way, but with training the mind becomes sharper, and so, as we made these marches, less of importance was missed.

During one of these observation marches, we were on the outskirts of a village, and an old man was working at the roadside; he was very affable, and started to walk alongside us, gesticulating and shouting pleasantries. Not understanding a word of what he was talking about, we answered him in English. Our language puzzled him just as his language puzzled us, and as the old man left us, one of our men shouted to him, 'It's a nice day, don't it?', to which the old man responded, '*vive l'Angleterre!*' Lieutenant Van Someren was highly amused by these exchanges and although he tried to suppress his laughter it eventually got the better of him and came out in an explosion of guffaws, as the rest of us joined in. In those days it was highly unusual for an officer to be seen, especially out in public, laughing with his men. The strictest formality was usually the order of the day.

There was another side to Van Someren too. He possessed a kind of courage that I thought was unique for the time. It was not the 'they shall not pass' kind of bravery (during the Second World War it was known as 'gung-ho'); he had a quiet, determined courage to do his duty at all costs, even though inside, like the rest of us, he was as frightened as a rabbit. Show me a man who was *not* as frightened as a rabbit in the kind of situations we found ourselves in during the Great War and I will show you a liar. Flesh and blood could not stand up to high explosive and cold steel, and I don't believe a man has yet been born who can face those things without fear. But Van Someren seemed always able to maintain a calm exterior, which gave strength to his men, and I was proud to be alongside such a man in times of stress.

To illustrate another story about Van Someren, first I need to explain a little about our situation at that time. As I have mentioned before, there were four machine guns to a section and these were spaced out along the firing line at varying intervals, sometimes 300–400 yards apart: one section could cover a front of half a mile or more (with soldiers from other units in between, of course). A section officer was supposed to visit each gun a certain number of times every 24 hours. One or other of the guns could be bombarded at any time, but it was only in a general attack that all the guns would be bombarded at the same time. So, it was policy for the officer to remain with a gun that was not under fire, waiting until a bombardment was over before moving on to the next.

There was an occasion near Lens when my gun position was under heavy fire. It was daytime and the man on sentry was a reinforcement, inexperienced and very frightened. I could understand his fear and took pity on him, and sent him down to the dugout, telling him that I would keep sentry until the shelling slackened off, not expecting that an officer would come while the situation was so hot. Then, to my surprise, I saw Van Someren approaching. He was trembling and obviously frightened himself, but it did not prevent him from doing his duty. His voice was a little shaky as he told me off for doing the sentry's job. He asked me why I did it, and I told him it was because the man had no previous experience of shelling and that I was sorry for him. He said 'Get him up here at once! What do you think will happen if the Germans attack and you, the leader, are out of action?'

So, I called the man up from the dugout to resume his sentry duty, and Van Someren stayed a little longer. After he had gone, someone said 'Well, that was a turn up for the book, fancy him coming at a time like this. We've got to hand it to the man – he's got guts.'

My action in doing the sentry's job was not entirely altruistic, however. By that stage, I was heartily sick – like many others – of being stuck in a stationary position, seeing men killed or maimed every day. My mind, I suppose, was in a state of fatalistic resignation that it was only a matter of time before the same happened to me, and my hope in relieving that sentry was that I might receive a 'Blighty One', a wound that was not too serious but enough to take me back to England, like a broken arm or leg.

We had a song which summed up the situation quite nicely:

Take me back to dear old Blighty
Put me on the train for London town
Take me over there
Drop me anywhere
Birmingham, Leeds or Man-ches-ter
Well, I don't care
I want to see my best girl
Cuddling up again, we soon shall be – hee
Hi-tee-hiddely-hi-tee
Take me back to Blighty
Blighty is the place for me

Although Van Someren censured me for doing the sentry's job, he had me promoted to full corporal (2 stripes) when we next got out of the trenches. This meant I would now get two shillings a day instead of one.

When I had first been made up to lance corporal I was sent on a three-week course of bayonet fighting. We had been paid the night before the course; my pay was five francs. Realising that it had to last me three weeks, I tried to increase it by having a flutter on the 'Crown and Anchor' board which a couple of the boys operated. Sadly, my luck was not in. I had gambled away three of my precious five francs before I came to my senses. I had to begin my three week course with only two francs in my pocket – what a prospect! Three of us did the course: one officer (2nd Lieutenant Miller) his batman, and myself. Needless to say, I spent all my remaining money on the first evening; it was such a nice change to be in a pleasant little town rather than the squalor of the trenches, I couldn't help myself. I remember there being a lovely aroma about the place (I forget the name of the town now) and we discovered it came from a small brewery near our camp. The aroma was fermenting hops and malt, a wholesome smell to our nostrils after the stench of fear and death.

There were about 200 men on the bayonet fighting course, representing every unit in the 6th Division. It was an intensive course and we were kept hard at it each and every day except Sundays. On the final day a prize was awarded for the man gaining the most points in a strenuous exercise with a number of dummies. Each dummy had a white circular sticker on it where the bayonet was supposed to penetrate. Some of the dummies were hung from ropes, some on the ground and some in trenches, the stickers placed in such positions to bring out the maximum effort on the soldier's part. The prize was twenty francs – or that was what we had heard.

I was lucky enough to gain the highest number of points and won the prize – which on that occasion (not so luckily) had been reduced to fifteen francs. Nevertheless, it was very welcome. As it was the last evening I fully intended to make up for lost time, and suffice it to say, I made a significant hole in the fifteen francs that night. I remarked to Lieutenant Miller how ironic it was that I had been broke since the first night of the course, and now it was time to go back, I was wealthy.

'You mean to say you've been here for three weeks with no money?' he said.

'That's quite right, Sir,' I replied.

'What a lousy time you must have had. Why on earth didn't you tell me?'

'Well, Sir,' I said, 'I did mention it several times to your batman, but he didn't seem very interested.'

You see, officers' servants, or batmen, were not a particularly comradely lot. They usually took on the job to avoid being sent to the trenches, at least that was my opinion, right or wrong. Of course, they had to go into the trenches when there was a battle going on, but when it was static trench warfare, the batmen stayed behind to keep their officers' belongings in good order. Lieutenant Miller's batman knew very well that I was broke, and I asked him to mention it to Miller. He said he would, but he obviously did not.

When we got back to the Company it was pay day again, and this time we were getting ten francs. When my turn came, the paying officer gave me my ten francs, and just as I was about to give him the salute, he said, 'Just a moment. I have orders here from the Commanding Officer to give you a further ten francs for upholding the honour of the Company in the bayonet-fighting competition.'

Now, I was definitely in the money! I couldn't wait to spend it. As we were in an area where there were still some civilians, I was looking forward to a good time for the remainder of my spell out of the trenches; we had nearly a week of our rest left. But, it was not to be. The next day, orders came through from Divisional HQ for us to return to the trenches that night. I had something like twenty francs in my pocket when we went back to the trenches. If only I could have had that much three weeks previously – but, such is life, as they say.

So, once again, we were back in the trenches. Our particular gun position was strategically placed between the first and second line of trenches, and was supposed to be 'secret'. It was camouflaged well to look like nothing was there, and we were told not to move about during daylight hours in case we were spotted by the German observation balloons. I always thought the OBs looked like enormous legless elephants in the sky. From the 'elephant' was suspended a basket containing the observer who spotted out our positions and directed artillery fire. Our side did the same, of course. We called them 'Blimps'.

It was possible to make out the shape of the fighting line by the way the Blimps were situated: ours on one side, the Jerries on the other, suspended in the air a mile or so behind the actual firing lines. The Blimps were tethered to heavy motor vehicles on the ground, and the job of the observer was a hazardous one. It was a common sight to witness a plane come over and shoot down the Blimps.

Our job in this secret position was to open fire only in the event of the front line being overrun by the enemy, and thus take them by surprise. But, as Rabbie Burns said: 'The best laid plans of mice an' men often gang agley.' – or words to that effect anyway. The secrecy of our position was betrayed by one of our own brigadiers, and not just any old brigadier commander of the line, but one from the General Staff no less, with his bright red epaulets, swagger stick and shiny, freshly polished insignia. He had two officer companions with him and he had decided to 'honour' us with a visit.

As there was no communicating trench to our position, he had, of necessity, to climb out of the approach trench and walk across open ground to us, an action which no man in his senses would have attempted in daylight. As he jumped into our trench, followed by his two mates, he asked, 'Who's in charge here?' I said that I was.

'You're machine gunners, aren't you?' he said.

'Yes, Sir,' I replied, thinking he wasn't very bright, and began to explain that our gun position was secret, so that we could surprise the enemy in the event the front line was overrun.

He more or less ignored me, and pointed with his swagger stick to a cloud. He said, 'See that cloud up there?'

'Yes, Sir,' I replied.

'ACTION!' he shouted.

Now I *knew* he wasn't very bright. The command 'action' required us to mount the gun and fire at the target indicated; however we had always been taught that a range-finding instrument would not be able to register the distance to a cloud. I was surprised at this command from such a high-ranking officer, and felt that I must say something.

'I beg your pardon, Sir,' I said, 'but it's not possible to get the range of a cloud on our instrument.' I could see immediately that he was furious that I had dared to question his order. He belonged to the 'Yours not to reason why, yours but to do or die' school, obviously, and it had made him very angry that his judgment had been called into question by a mere corporal.

'Get that gun into action!' he bawled.

I had no choice but to obey him. So we mounted the gun as best we could to fire at his cloud; this was not easy as a special structure would normally be required to fire such a gun straight up into the air. Then, in accordance with his instructions, we opened fire on the cloud. It was madness! If our position had not been spotted before that moment, we knew it certainly would be now. He left our trench soon afterwards, by the same method as he had come, taking his chums with him, and leaving us to face the aftermath. And it wasn't long before the Jerries began pasting us with everything they had. It was only by pure luck that none of us was seriously hurt – a scratch or two from flying debris was all we sustained – but no thanks to our brigadier.

I can think of no valid reason to this day why this high-ranking officer should have acted in such a foolhardy way. However, I can think of three *invalid* reasons. He might have come to show off his 'knowledge' of machine gunnery to us and his mates. Or, he might have just been a bully (there were plenty of those) who wanted to vent his spleen on people who were in no position to hit back. If either was the case, then his actions were vain and stupid indeed, as all he showed off was his *lack* of knowledge of machine gunnery, and his behaviour could have got us all killed, himself and his friends included. The third possibility, and this last explanation seemed to me to be the most likely, was that there were people in High Command, and he could have been one of them, who did not agree with the formation of our 'newfangled' unit – the Machine Gun Corps – believing that the old traditional Army deployments were better. So, he could have 'had it in for us' and had come to throw his weight about. In a war of extinction, as the Great War was, one would hardly think there would be rivalry between regular Army personnel and the patriotic army of civilians, but it did indeed exist. The rivalry, though, was generally not unfriendly, but rather like the attitude of the professional towards the amateur, as in most walks of life.

Of course, the regular soldier was miles ahead of us in the knowledge of Army rules and regulations, and often helped us when it came to a question of procedure, but when we were in the trenches there was no distinction, as this kind of warfare was as new to them as it was to us. As we faced the dangers and privations of trench life together, we grew to trust each other, and I always felt that each was proud to be associated with the other; yet there was a core of die-hards too stiff-necked to accept anything new, and among these, I suspect, was our visiting brigadier. His actions, though, could still have got us all killed.

All of our Company officers were of the new 'civilian' army, and most were very fine men. Our Company Commander was a Scotsman, a grand leader and a humanitarian, who always gave credit where it was due. In his presence you felt that he instilled confidence and he would often turn a blind eye to petty misdemeanours. Unfortunately, we lost him on the Somme; he was invalided home with the dreaded trench fever. I am sorry to say that I don't remember his name now, only his character and personality. Perhaps it is not so strange really that I don't remember his name, for these memories are over 50 years old. It is the incidents and experiences that remain impressed so vividly on my mind. I don't want to invent names; I want to record only actual experiences, and there are many of the Great War which are so imprinted on my memory that I shall remember them as long as I live.

CHAPTER SEVEN

SOMME OFFENSIVE – BATTLE OF FLERS

On 1 July 1916 the Battle of the Somme commenced. There was terrible carnage: nearly 20,000 British soldiers dead on the first day alone, another 40,000 wounded. The resistance of the Germans was so great that an advance of the line of 200–300 yards was deemed a great victory. The news of this new Allied offensive, and rumours of the slaughter, spread to us in the Ypres Salient and we at once began to wonder how long it would be before it would be our turn to join in. Week after week went by amid rumour and speculation. We didn't know it then, of course, but the call was to come about the middle of August.

Until then, still in the Ypres Salient, we had a little time on our hands, the shooting and shelling quieter than it had been since we first arrived. I recall one day, when I was using the time to write a letter home, I was doodling on my writing pad, making some sketches of this and that, when an idea came to me about 'indirect firing'. This was a part of machine gun practice in which we were well schooled; it meant firing at a target which couldn't be seen, carried out by magnetic compass and maps. Entrenched as the two armies were, we had done a lot of 'indirect firing', chiefly at night, and it involved a certain amount of risk, as it would take us ten minutes or more to switch targets. My idea, I reckoned, could minimise this risk, by enabling us to switch to any target within our range in a few seconds. I sketched it out on my pad and then showed it to Lieutenant Van Someren. He thought it was a splendid idea and said he would show it to the CO when we got out of the trenches.

This he did. He told me that the CO had also thought it a good idea, but that 'High Command are planning to abolish trench warfare' as it was felt that to achieve a break-through of the German lines the troops needed to get out of the trenches and fight in open country. As my idea was only applicable to trench warfare and would be useless in open warfare, that was that, which was a pity, as trench warfare was certainly not abolished in 1916!

Towards the end of August 1916, when the Battle of the Somme had been raging for six weeks, our Division was relieved by another, quite suddenly. It was obvious there was some urgency to it, as, in the ordinary way, we should have had some inkling of it. So, although we had been expecting to move from that particular front, the suddenness surprised us to say the least. It must also have surprised Headquarters, for they had sent all stores on ahead, so that when we got back to HQ there was no food for us. We had no supper that night, nor did we have any breakfast next morning before a long march off to an unknown destination. We didn't stop until after midday, when we were indeed tired and hungry men.

I must mention here that every soldier should have had with him an emergency ration, known as 'iron rations', which consisted of a muslin bag containing a quantity of small, round biscuits and a tin of bully beef. I suppose that on that day the 'powers that be' thought we still had these rations with us, as it was forbidden to eat them except in an emergency. Well, the 'powers that be' were wrong! Those iron rations had all been eaten long ago; the little biscuits, being easy to chew, made a nice but temporary substitute for bread, and we never felt it necessary to carry just a tin of bully beef as they were always readily available, or so we thought.

We had arrived at our rendezvous very hungry. What wouldn't we have given at that moment for 'just a tin of bully'! We still had to wait some time for the lorries to arrive to take us down to the Somme. The fact that we were being transported by lorry instead of 'Shanks's pony' was an indication of the urgency of our situation. The stores, guns, mules and limbers had already been put on a train and had moved off. Soon after, the lorries arrived and we boarded them, about ten to a lorry.

When we were all aboard and we started moving off, we divided ourselves into two fives, the intention being that every man should thoroughly search his kit in the hope of finding something, anything, resembling food, and if anyone found anything it was to be shared among his five. In my five, a small tin of jam was found. We each got a spoon out of our kit and, in turn, took a spoonful until the tin was empty. That must have been the cleanest jam tin ever.

The journey seemed to take an eternity, but eventually we arrived at our destination – by that time thoroughly starving hungry – and we then had to unload all our stores, ammunition, mules etc. We had been promised a meal only when all these chores had been completed.

As we were marching from the lorries to the sidings, we passed over a railway bridge. On the bridge was a woman standing beside a trestle table on which was piled a small pyramid of little cakes. Lieutenant Van Someren halted us while he talked to the woman; in the end, he bought the lot. There were just enough for one cake each with a few left over – and any one of us could have eaten them all. It was a fine gesture, though, on the officer's part, and I'm sure it was appreciated by all of us, but one tiny cake did little to allay the hunger of nearly 30 hours standing; on the contrary, it seemed to rouse the sleeping pangs of hunger into an almost frenzied desire for food. Nevertheless, we thought Van Someren was a great bloke.

Eventually, after we had finished the unloading, we were given a meal of stew made with bully beef and Machonachie rations, and never was a meal more eagerly devoured – it was the Lord Mayor's banquet, the Feeding of the Five Thousand and the Boy Scouts' Jamboree all rolled into one.

We thought, because of the panic of getting us down to the Somme so quickly, that we would be going into action immediately, but this was not so. Of course, we knew nothing of what the 'top brass' had in mind at the time (we never knew what they had in mind at *any* time), although we learned afterwards that our Division, along with several others, was to receive special training, the object being to achieve a break-through of the German lines to enable the cavalry to push through and make the Germans fight in open country. And there was to be a 'secret weapon': the tank.

This first version of the tank was a clumsy looking monster, with caterpillar tracks, two great wheels at the back to steer it, and a large bale of brushwood carried on the top, to be dropped into any deep hole it might encounter in its path. Without those two large wheels for steering, the tank could not turn or deviate from a straight line; they performed the same function as a ship's rudder, and the first name we knew these vehicles by was 'Land Ship'. We were to see our first tank only the day before we went into action with them.

Our special training began. We were subjected to intensive physical training, battle practice and discipline, and we knew we were going to be in for a hot time. It was impressed upon us that once we had gone 'over the top' and started to advance, any man turning back would be shot. This even applied to men assisting any wounded back to the dressing station. It was emphasised again and again to us that however badly a wounded man needed attention we must ignore him completely – or we'd be shot. The wounded, we were told, would be taken care of by the medical units and stretcher-bearers who would be following behind the battle units.

On 14 September 1916, we moved up to the front and had our first glimpses of the Land Ships with which we were to go into action the next day, which was, of course, the memorable 15 September and the Battle of Flers. We had moved up during the night to specified positions, with full instructions as to our objective, and to stop and 'dig in' on reaching it, and allow other units following behind to pass through us to continue the advance. During the night of the 14th, all watches had to be synchronised so that everyone would do what he had to do at the precise moment he should do it. We all knew the time the bombardment would start and the time we would go 'over the top', and it is a question which was the more terrifying – the tenseness of the waiting or the actual fact of going into action. I still remember vividly how agitated everyone was, faces flushed and eyes staring wildly with fear for what might be in store for them in the next few hours, all hoping that their name was not on any of the projectiles about to be released by the enemy. I have said it before: any man who says he is not afraid in moments like these is either a fool or a liar, or both.

The dawn of the 15th finally arrived and the bombardment started. To say that 'all hell was let loose' doesn't even begin to describe that first day. Just the noise of it was enough to send a man insane. It was a good thing that every man knew what his job was, so that no further orders were necessary, because they would never have been heard above the thunderous din.

The countdown ticked away and eventually it was time for us to go 'over the top'. We climbed out of our trench with the guns and ammunition and started moving forward. We could see the tanks going ahead of us; it must have been a terrifying sight for the Germans to see those huge monsters lumbering towards them, but they tried very bravely to fight them off with machine-gun fire. Shells were bursting all around us and I could see men falling to the right and left of us, but we kept moving forward, expecting to share their fate at any moment.

About half-way to our first objective, I saw a Grenadier Guardsman lying in a shallow trench. His wounds were horrific. Our eyes met as we passed and the look in his eyes compelled me to stop for a moment. He asked me to help him, and begged me to get him out of there. I felt so sorry for him, but all I could do for him was to give him a drink of water and tell him what he undoubtedly knew already: that I would be shot if I left the battlefield, so I couldn't help him. I tried to buoy him up by saying, 'Cheer up, mate, you'll be alright, the Red Cross will come to you soon', but it was hard to keep the hopelessness out of my voice. I had no choice but to move on and catch up with my comrades and continue pushing forward until we reached our objective.

All day long the bombardment continued on both sides, and all around us were dead and dying men – it was like Dante's Inferno. We were soaked to the skin with the blood of our comrades. We could see several of the tanks which had been knocked out by enemy fire, lying derelict. At the end of the day, the advance had moved on – how far I do not recall – but we did not break through as had been hoped; however, it was still the biggest advance so far.

All night long and all the next day, we were subjected to counter bombardments from the Germans. Soon, I was the only one of the gun team who had not become a casualty, the other five having been wounded and taken away. I began to believe I had a charmed life.

When darkness fell on the night of the 16th, I was visited by a scouting party from Company Headquarters who were rounding up what was left of the Company and I was told to assemble at a certain spot where we would meet a Lieutenant Pickering who would guide us back to camp. My first question on meeting Lieutenant Pickering was, 'Is Davies alright, Sir?' He told me he was and already back in camp. Then he added, 'That's strange, you know. His first question to me was to ask the same thing about you.'

The camp was sufficiently far back and low lying that a fire was permitted by the CO and, as our party approached, I could see men sitting around it, among whom I recognised my old pal and best comrade, Garnet Davies. He did not look up or show any interest in our party until we actually arrived. I saw him glance round casually as I approached, his face clearly visible in the firelight, whilst mine was still in darkness: I could see him but he couldn't see me. Then suddenly he saw me. He jumped up and came over to me; we clasped hands and shook each other's vigorously, both talking at the same time. When he had a chance, he said, 'I've been as miserable as hell about you. They told me you'd got killed!' He was obviously as glad to see me as I was to see him, as this was the first time I had ever seen Garn show emotion – he was normally a stoical man. I told him that I hadn't heard any news at all about anyone else as we seemed to have been isolated from the rest of the Company.

It was so good to be reunited with my pal that we talked and talked well into the night. We finally fell to sleep with the sky for a blanket –

this was not a camp in the true sense, just somewhere to rest for a while, and we had to lie where we could with only our greatcoats to cover us. While we were asleep it started to rain, but we were quite oblivious to it until it eventually woke us when we were saturated and lying in about two or three inches of water. We got up and went in search of shelter. It was daylight by this time, and we found that we were in a kind of sunken road with embankments on either side. On one side were old dugouts, large enough to accommodate about four men, the nearer ones being already occupied by men who had not been talking half the night as we had been. We found one at last with only two occupants and settled in.

We managed to get a fire going and eventually dried out our clothes during the day, and, as we had no duties to perform, we walked around making enquiries about how the other men had fared. Their stories were much the same as ours, and we learned that we had lost 71 officers, NCOs and men in the battle – more than half our total strength. This, we later discovered, was about average for most units engaged on the Somme.

This appalling loss of life was taken for granted in the newspapers, which reached us several days late. The headlines would indicate that the Germans had killed fewer of our men than we had killed of theirs – a 'very satisfactory situation', it seemed. Headlines such as 'All Quiet On The Western Front' would occasionally appear, and the text underneath would predictably run something like this: 'There was little activity on the Western Front yesterday except for a local action in the vicinity of -----, where our troops took a line of trenches and inflicted heavy losses on the enemy.' It would usually add that our losses had been 'slight'. I have no doubt that German newspapers were telling their readers the same lies but in reverse.

It was sometimes grimly amusing to read of one of those 'local actions' in which we had been involved; believe me, they were quite different in reality from the newspaper reports. Yet, we swallowed all the good things they said about 'our gallant troops', proud to be described as 'gallant'. We still believed that God was on our side and that after the war there would be no more war. I believe it was David Lloyd George who made the famous quote that 'This war is the war to end war.' ['I hope we may say that this fateful morning, came to an end all wars.' Speech in the House of Commons, 11 November 1918.]

Looking back now, over the fifty-odd years, it occurs to me how gullible we were to believe it. I wonder now where all the men of God were, the prelates, philosophers and men of letters, during the First World War. These men must have known of the terrible slaughter that was going on, so why did they let the war, which decimated an entire generation of young men, continue? Education, substance and opportunity produce great men, so it is said; well, they also produce fools. There were many 'great men', on both sides, conducting this war, yet there were none sufficiently 'great' to end the dreadful bloodbath.

I will even venture to say that just one ordinary soldier from each country, with an interpreter, could have settled it in less than 24 hours by talking across a table. I advance this theory on the actual facts of what happened on the Western Front during the Christmas truce of 1914. I was not yet in the Army at that time, but I remember there was much publicity about it. The troops of both sides came out of their trenches, exchanged greetings, even Christmas gifts, and then played an impromptu game of football in no man's land. There had been no hatred then. It was an example simply of the wish of the common man, from both sides, to be friendly and have done with killing. Yet, they were killing each other again the next day, after being admonished by the 'High ups' for fraternising.

I was not sufficiently worldly-wise (or cynical?) to have had these thoughts at the time; maybe the reason I have these thoughts now is because, having reached old age, I can sit back and contemplate these truly awful events from a different perspective.

One would have thought at least that the lessons of the 1914–18 war would have taught the world's leaders the futility of it all – but, no. Only twenty years later they were at it again as the Second World War raged across Europe, Africa and Asia. As I write this, in the year 1967, there is another war, this time in Vietnam, also in the Middle East and various uprisings in Africa – all because of power-drunk leaders. What I do know is that no peoples of any country are ever consulted about whether or not they think it is right to go to war, and yet they are the ones who have to fight them – and sacrifice their lives. Having seen at first hand the absolutely futile carnage of war, I think what a pity it is that some scheme has never been evolved whereby all propaganda is abolished and the peoples of the world persuade their leaders to talk instead of fight – for that, in the end, is what has to be done.

CHAPTER EIGHT

HOME LEAVE – THIRD BATTLE OF YPRES – PASSCHENDAELE

After the Battle of Flers, for whatever reason I do not know, I have no recollection as to exactly where we went or what we did for the next few months. I can only think that the horrors of that battle, the sights I witnessed, and the deafening, ceaseless cacophony of noise, were enough to blot it all from my mind. I do remember, though, that in 1916, my two younger brothers, Tom and Edgar, joined up: Tom in the Merchant Navy and Edgar in the Royal Navy. I remember how this news saddened me, as I thought of my Dad and how worried he and the rest of the family would be.

The only other clear memories of that time were of two further actions which I was involved in before we left the Somme. The bloodiest of these was at Beaumont Hamel, which was, if anything, worse than Flers. At Flers we could at least move about; at Beaumont Hamel we were restricted to a defensive role and were more or less stationary because of the intense bombardment directed at our lines both day and night. And if ever a man earned a Victoria Cross it was a certain William MacCormack, an Irishman from Tipperary. He carried messages between the front line and forward HQ for six days and nights, under heavy fire all the time. The communication trench was about seven feet deep at the start, but during the incessant six day and night bombardment, it acquired a series of shell holes, the large craters of which rendering the trench quite unrecognisable. Yet, that man delivered every message both to the front line from HQ and HQ back to the front line, catching only a little sleep at odd times during the whole of the period. (Incidentally, the question of sleep at times like this is something which I will try to explain a little later.) William MacCormack came through his ordeal without a scratch, which, perversely, was probably the reason he was not recommended for a medal.

After the Battle of Flers, where we lost more than half our Company, we had to be reinforced before going into action at Beaumont Hamel. Among those reinforcements I remember one man in particular. He was a good type, a well set up man, pleasant and intelligent. This was his first time under fire, and I, remembering my own 'first time' in Ypres, could understand well how anxious he was feeling. However, compared to Beaumont Hamel, Ypres had been like a Sunday afternoon in the park. The poor devil! After two days and nights of constant German shell-fire, he had to be taken away, completely deranged and babbling like a sick child.

I do not remember exactly how long we occupied this sector, but I do remember that we had to spend two days and nights in the trenches, then one day and night in reserve throughout the period. The reserve lines lay in a hollow and could not be seen from the enemy lines, so we could move about fairly freely. During one of our rest days, three or four of us were off scrounging firewood along an old railway line, when we had the surprise of our lives. An officer suddenly appeared as if from nowhere, giving us a fright. He asked us the way to the front line. We pointed it out to him, wondering why anyone who didn't have to be on the front line would *want* to go up and visit it. After he had gone out of earshot, we suddenly looked at each other, and then looked at each other again, disbelieving what, or rather *who* we had seen. It was the Prince of Wales!

We had to admire his bravery for wishing to go up to the front, particularly as no-one would have blamed him if he had stayed safely tucked away in England. He was a similar age to me, perhaps a bit younger, in his twenties. His aides must have been worried stiff as to where he had got to, but he had a reputation even then for his habit of going off on his own to 'see things for himself'. Later, during the Depression, I recall him visiting South Wales, where he promptly discarded the conducted tour which had been arranged for him and insisted on seeing things as they really were. The Prince of Wales became very popular for his 'common touch'. Personally, I admired him greatly ever since our encounter at Beaumont Hamel, for, to my mind, it was an act of sheer physical courage to go into those trenches when he need not have done; it was like volunteering for an excursion to Hell itself. Later, I thought he had moral courage too, when he gave up his kingship to marry the woman he loved. That was my opinion, anyway.

Beaumont Hamel was one battle that still stands out clearly in my mind from that time; a battle near Bapaume is another. The battle near Bapaume was noteworthy for me for the fact that the existence of God was proved to me on that first terrible morning.

We were to attack at dawn; all watches had been synchronised. The hours before the battle went by, as they always did, with increasing trepidation, until we came to the last half hour or so. Half an hour to go! Fifteen minutes to go! Ten minutes to go! The tension becomes unbearable. You see the faces of your fellow soldiers become flushed and drawn with both fear and excitement. Two minutes to go! It was at that point that all fear left me. I became tranquil and imbued suddenly with the absolute knowledge that I would not be hurt that day. This conviction was not merely wishful thinking; it was *certainty*. I knew absolutely that I would not be hurt. Like an actor, who knows in advance what will happen in a play, having learned the lines beforehand, I was just as certain that I knew the outcome of the battle for me: I would survive it.

One minute to go! All along the trench everybody was poised to make the leap over the top and advance. Then, we heard the whistles blow and over we went, and the attack was underway.

How far we advanced, or how many men we lost that day, I do not recall. I only know that I went forward without a shred of fear – yet two minutes before the attack I had been just as frightened as everyone else. Now, cynics may say that my lack of fear was due to the effects of the rum ration (a potent brew which bore no resemblance to the rum sold in public houses) which was always issued just before we went over the top, sometimes a double ration, but I would tell them categorically that they were wrong. Why? Because I never took my rum ration that day; like my comrade Garn Davies always used to say, 'If I am to die, I will die sober.' Not, of course that I was against the rum ration. I always enjoyed my nips of rum at other times. But I believed that, on that day, God had decided to protect me. And he did a good job of it, because I survived that very bloody battle completely unscathed.

It was towards the end of 1916 that I received a parcel from home. Amongst other things there was a cake, and inside the cake was a golden half sovereign, just in time for Christmas. The half sovereign had been sent by my older brother Albert. The gesture filled me with an almost overwhelming homesickness, the desire to see him and the rest of my family again was intense, but they seemed a million miles away. It was now nearly a year since I had left home, and it seemed a lifetime.

There was a small ray of hope of some home leave, though, around that time. Orders had come through that two men at a time could go home on leave, the two men returning before the next two could go. Unfortunately, it was to be in alphabetical order, and as my surname began with 'R', I knew I would have to wait some time – six months to be precise, as my turn didn't come until the beginning of July 1917.

I remember that leave well. As soon as I was told I could go – ten days leave! – I knew there would not be time to let them know at home: preparations were too hectic for that. I left the trenches and went back to Company HQ where I was given a new set of underwear, my thoroughly louse-ridden clothes discarded and sent away for fumigation, a new uniform, 100 francs and a shower – pure, unadulterated bliss!

The next morning, my companion and I set off for Boulogne by general service wagon, which was horse-drawn, as far as Hazebrouck, then by train to Boulogne. In Boulogne there was a two or three hour wait before we were allowed on the ship – we could see it in the harbour – and it felt wonderful to be free to saunter around to pass the time. We found a grassy bank nearby and we lay down, enjoying the warm sun. It was a lovely, hot summer day and we lay in the sun hoping to get a tan, but I got more than I bargained for. I fell asleep, and when I woke up my face was as red as a beetroot and very sore.

On board at last and homeward bound, we had a calm sea and very few seasick passengers – how different from my previous crossing. If the danger of being torpedoed entered our minds, it was pushed aside by the confidence we had in our naval guardians, who were always keenly alert. (I am not quite sure but I think not a single cross-channel troopship was lost throughout the whole war, which is a fine tribute to the vigilance of our naval comrades.) There was an easy camaraderie between the passengers, all servicemen; we mixed freely, as though we had known each other all our lives, due, no doubt, to the mutual horrors we had experienced.

We reached England safely and were at London's Victoria Station by late afternoon. There we were met by special guides wearing arm bands, who steered us to the stations most suitable for our various destinations. I was soon on a train to Birmingham which would go via Banbury. I mention Banbury because it was there the train stopped long enough for us to get a snack. We were feeling very hungry, having had no time for lunch on our travels. We had changed our French money at Victoria Station in anticipation of buying ourselves some food – we were in for a pleasant surprise. As we pulled into Banbury, a bevy of beautiful girls awaited us! They had set up tables on the platform with tea, cakes and rolls. It was an enchanting sight. They waited on us most attentively, and talked to us the whole time in very flattering terms, telling us how brave we were, and hoping we would have a happy homecoming, and a safe return from the war. These girls were 'doing their bit' for the war by providing this service to all servicemen passing through. It was a good morale-boosting operation and much appreciated by me I'm sure!

On reaching Birmingham, I was on the final leg of my long journey home. I had to catch a local train to Walsall, then walk down to the Bridge, which was the tram terminus, to board the tram to Bloxwich. Having my full pack with me, all 90 pounds of it, including rifle but no ammunition, I elected to go on the top deck and sit on that quadrangular seat at the back. There was a teenage boy sitting there already; I paid little attention to him at first, but as the tram got underway, I was surprised to hear him say, 'Hello, Uncle Ted.' I was quite startled and stared at him.

'Well, well,' I said, 'I shouldn't have known you if you hadn't spoken.' It was young Len, my brother Len's eldest son. It was a year and a half since I had last seen him and he had grown very tall – it made me realise just how long I had been away.

We talked all the way to Bloxwich and both got off at the Pinfold. When we were a few hundred yards from home, I began to worry that the shock of my sudden appearance might be too much for Dad, as I had been unable to warn him of my home leave. So, I told young Len what I feared and asked him to run on and tell his granddad that he *thought* Uncle Ted *might* be coming up the road, to prepare Dad for the shock.

When I walked in, what a welcome I had! My dear old Dad, despite the 'advance warning' from Len, had to sit down to regain his composure. When he had eventually calmed himself, I learned how young Len had broken the news. Far from breaking it gently, like I had told him to, he had burst into the house yelling at the top of his voice, 'Uncle Ted's coming! Uncle Ted's coming!' So much for breaking it gently.

My first reunion with my family was joyous. My only regret was that Tom and Edgar were not there too, although, by a remarkable coincidence, Edgar was expected in a few days for a 48-hour leave. Ada, practical as ever, soon had a meal ready for me, and what a lovely change it was to eat sitting at a table with a white tablecloth and clean cutlery and my family around me.

Before going to bed that night, I wrote to my fiancée, Agnes, who lived near my relatives in Merthyr Tydfil, South Wales, to tell her I was home on leave, and that I would be arriving to fetch her up to my home the day after tomorrow, so that she could stay with us during my leave. We had been engaged about two years, although I had seen precious little of her in that time. I had wanted to get married before joining up, but she thought it would be better to wait until the war was over.

I went to South Wales, as promised, to see my fiancée. Unfortunately, she didn't seem keen on coming back with me. She wanted me to spend my leave with her in South Wales, but I wanted to see my family too, as I had been away for so long. Anyway, we ended up having quite a row, until she reluctantly agreed to come back with me the next day. Having gained my point, I nevertheless felt that everything was not as it should be, but I couldn't define it. I hoped I was mistaken, as I was in love with her; Agnes was a very interesting person, intelligent and witty and always immaculately dressed.

On Merthyr Tydfil station, I looked up and down the waiting train to find an empty compartment where I hoped we could do a little 'necking', but it was not to be. There were other passengers with us all the way home. In these days (1967) the presence of other passengers would not really present a problem, but in 1917 we had to be more circumspect. Kissing and cuddling in public would have been condemned as outrageous and scandalous behaviour. We made up for lost time, however, during the rest of my leave.

The last evening was spent visiting relatives and friends and saying goodbye, and, on looking back, it seems ironic that Agnes should have met and made friends on that evening with Edie Parton, the woman I eventually married; although neither she nor I had the slightest inkling of it at that time – which just goes to show that we never know what fate has in store for us. (Edie was at that time married to the brother of my brother Ernie's wife – if you can work that one out.) Our visits over, Agnes and I took the longest way round to get home, had a bit of supper and talked with the family. When everyone else had gone up to bed, Agnes and I stayed up until the early hours, kissing and cuddling, and making the most of the time left to us. But again I had that feeling that something was not quite as it should be.

I got up at about 7.30 as I wanted to have a bath before the girls got up, for I had no idea when I should get another chance. Our house had no bathroom, but I boiled a couple of saucepans and a kettle of water, then took the old tin bath into the middle room and had a quick sponge down. After breakfast it was time to go. Agnes was going home too; her train to South Wales leaving from Wolverhampton station, so I decided to catch my train from Wolverhampton too. My train was the first to leave; Agnes and I had a final embrace before the train pulled off. I leaned out of the window, waving to her until my train passed under a bridge and she was lost from sight. I did not know it at the time, but that was to be our final parting.

It was in a considerably more sombre mood than on my homeward journey that I began the long trip back to war. The Wolverhampton train was delayed on its way to London, and on arrival I discovered I had missed my connection, so I had no option but to stay in London overnight and catch the boat train to make the Channel crossing the next day. By the time I got back to my Company, I was two days late and worried I would be reprimanded for overstaying my leave. Fortunately, I had asked an officer of one of the units I had been travelling with to sign my pass, so I did not get into trouble.

Our Company had moved back to the Ypres Salient, and back in the trenches things were unusually quiet after the horrors of the Somme – the lull before the storm as it turned out. After about a week I began to receive letters from home once again. I had arranged a 'secret code' with Albert which would tell the family of my whereabouts, as it was strictly forbidden to mention in letters home the names of any places we happened to be. I was to write in my letter some sentences, the first letter of each sentence spelling out the name of the place. I was at Ypres, so my letter home went something like this:

Your letter received with thanks.
Please forgive me for not writing sooner.
Really, the weather is atrocious!
Expect me again when you see me.
Send word about Tom and Edgar.

Of course, the above is only an example, as I have not the faintest idea of what I actually wrote. It never got through though. It was not quite so obvious as the example I have given, but I must have been a bit naïve to have expected it to beat the hawk-eyed censors at HQ.

Back from my leave, I received two letters together; the first was from Albert, the second from Agnes. It always lifted the spirits to receive a

THE ROWBOTHAM FAMILY TREE

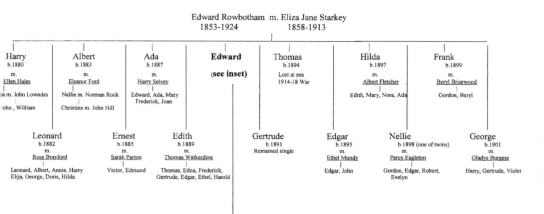

Edward Rowbotham m. Eliza Jane Starkey
1853-1924   1858-1913

Harry	Albert	Ada	**Edward**	Thomas	Hilda	Frank
b.1880	b.1883	b.1887	**(see inset)**	b.1894	b.1897	b.1899
m.	m.	m.		Lost at sea	m.	m.
Ellen Hales	Eleanor Ford	Harry Selvey		1914-18 War	Albert Fletcher	Beryl Briarwood
...a m. John Lowndes	Nellie m. Norman Rock	Edward, Ada, Mary			Edith, Mary, Nora, Ada	Gordon, Beryl
...ohn , William	Christine m. John Hill	Frederick, Joan				

Leonard	Ernest	Edith	Gertrude	Edgar	Nellie	George
b.1882	b.1885	b.1889	b.1891	b.1895	b.1898 (one of twins)	b.1901
m.	m.	m.	Remained single	m.	m.	m.
Rose Brayford	Sarah Parton	Thomas Walkerdine		Ethel Mundy	Percy Eagleton	Gladys Burgess
Leonard, Albert, Annie, Harry	Victor, Edmund	Thomas, Edna, Frederick,		Edgar, John	Gordon, Edgar, Robert,	Harry, Gertrude, Violet
Elija, George, Doris, Hilda		Gertrude, Edgar, Ethel, Harold			Evelyn	

Edward Rowbotham (1890-1973) m. Edith Parton (née Foxall)

Edith (1921-) m. Jack Powell

Sheila (1950-)   Janet (1955-)
m.   m.
Chris Harvey   Graham Tucker

Matthew (1980-)   Louise(1986-) David (1987-)

The Rowbotham family in 1902, all sixteen of them! This photograph was taken outside the house at The Quadrant, Green Lane, Leamore. Edward was twelve and is seated fourth from the right.

Above: High Street and Reeves Street, Bloxwich in the early 1900s. *(Courtesy of Walsall Local History Centre)*

Below: High Street, Bloxwich in 1913. *(Courtesy of Walsall Local History Centre)*

Above: Church Street, Bloxwich in the early 1900s. *(Walsall Local History Centre)*

Below: Church Street, Bloxwich today.

Opposite above: Two raw recruits with a Vickers machine gun. Although the provenance of this photograph is unknown, the neat appearance of the men implies that it may well have been taken at Grantham where men of the MCG trained before going to the front. It is of special interest because the man on the left bears an uncanny resemblance to Edward. *(Courtesy of Graham Sacker, MGC OCA)*

Opposite below: A young officer trains with a Vickers gun, possibly taken at Belton Park, Grantham. *(Courtesy of Paul Cutmore)*

Below: A group of officers of the Machine Gun Corps, possibly taken during training at Belton Park. *(Courtesy of Paul Cutmore)*

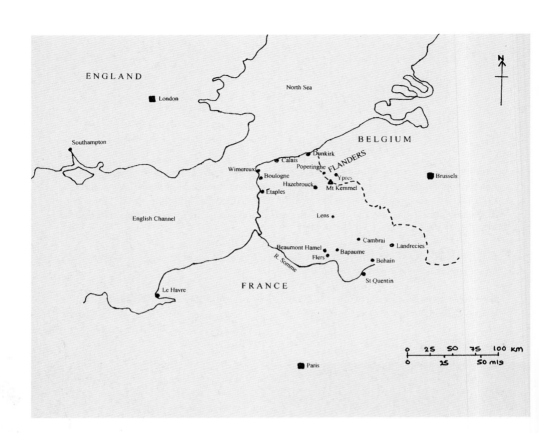

Above: Life in the trenches. Infantrymen on the Ypres Salient. *(Courtesy of The Staffordshire Regiment Museum)*

Opposite above: The Western Front.

Opposite below: Men of the 5th South Staffordshire Regiment on the march. Note the Vickers machine gun on the horse-drawn carriage. *(Courtesy of The Staffordshire Regiment Museum)*

Above: Infantrymen in a trench, showing a dugout at Hill 60, Ypres Salient. *(Courtesy of The Staffordshire Regiment Museum)*

Below: Men of the Staffordshire Regiment snatch forty winks in a trench, Ypres Salient. *(Courtesy of The Staffordshire Regiment Museum)*

TAKE ME BACK TO DEAR OLD BLIGHTY. (2)

Take me back to dear old Blighty, put me on the train
    for London town,
Take me over there, drop me anywhere,
Birmingham, Leeds, or Manchester—well, I don't care!
I should love to see my best girl, cuddling up again we
    soon shall be ;
Whoa ! Tiddley-iddley-ighty, hurry me home to Blighty—
    Blighty is the place for me.

BAMFORTH COPYRIGHT   WORDS BY PERMISSION OF THE STAR MUSIC PUBLISHING CO LONDON

A typical First World War postcard showing happy men in the trenches. It was supposed to be reassuring, if a little misleading, to family back home. *(Courtesy of Judith Lappin, MGC OCA)*

A postcard showing British troops in Poperinghe, near Ypres. *(Courtesy of Sheila Hilton)*

The ruins of Ypres. Edward described it as a desolate place, the skyline at night looking like a row of broken bottles on a wall. *(Courtesy of The Staffordshire Regiment Museum)*

Troops hurry to fit their gas masks during a gas alarm on the Ypres Salient. *(Courtesy of the Staffordshire Regiment Museum)*

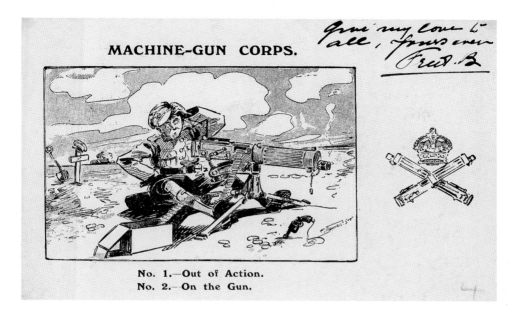

MACHINE-GUN CORPS.

Give my love to all, yours ever Fred .B.

No. 1.—Out of Action.
No. 2.—On the Gun.

ove: Postcard by Sergeant Fred Beauvais of the Machine Gun Corps, showing typical black trench humour. The
o. 1', who normally fires the gun is 'out of action' (note the grave), so 'No. 2' has to take over. Unfortunately
does not seem to have paid attention during his firing training. *(Courtesy of Andy Bray, MGC OCA)*

low: Two Machine Gun Corps postcards. *(Courtesy of Bill Fulton, MGC History Project)*

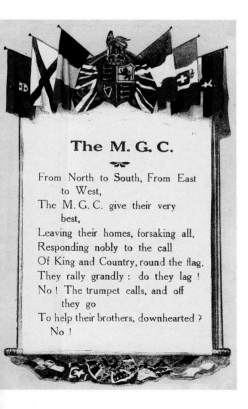

The M. G. C.

From North to South, From East
to West,
The M. G. C. give their very
best,
Leaving their homes, forsaking all,
Responding nobly to the call
Of King and Country, round the flag,
They rally grandly : do they lag !
No ! The trumpet calls, and off
they go
To help their brothers, downhearted ?
No !

SERVING KING
AND COUNTRY

M G C

From One of the
MACHINE GUN CORPS.

Above: A machine gun team firing at enemy aircraft, April 1917. *(IWM Q 5173)*

Below: The Third Battle of Ypres, 1917, showing the shell-torn, swamp-like conditions of the battlefield. *(IWM Q 6049)*

Above: The Somme battlefield, 1917, showing the remains of a Mk 1 tank from the Battle of Flers. Edward's machine gun company fought alongside these tanks when they were used for the first time at the Battle of Flers in September 1916. *(IWM Q 11617)*

Below: The Somme battlefield during the Battle of Cambrai, November 1917; men of the 6th Division, including machine gunners, in a captured trench. Edward's machine gun company was part of the 6th Division and fought at the Battle of Cambrai. *(IWM Q6279)*

M GC Records 3R 5/10/775

CERTIFICATE of * { ~~Discharge~~ / Transfer to Reserve / ~~Disembodiment~~ / ~~Demobilization~~ } on Demobilization.

Regtl. No. 6470 .... Rank ...... Sgt

Names in full ...... Rowbotham Edward
(Surname first)

Unit and Regiment or Corps
from which } 6th Bt MGCorps
*~~Discharged~~
Transferred to Reserve

Enlisted on the 1st November 1915

For .... 5th Stafford Regt
(Here state Regiment or Corps to which first appointed)

Also served in ....

.... Mt MGc ....

Only Regiments or Corps in which the Soldier served since August 4th, 1914, are to be stated. If inapplicable, this space is to be ruled through in ink and initialled.

† Medals and
Decorations
awarded during } Military Medal Lg/ 11-12-18
present engage-
ment

*Has
~~Has not~~ } served Overseas on Active Service.

Place of Rejoining in }
case of emergency } Clipstone   Medical Category A.1

Specialist Military }
qualifications } nil   Year of birth .. 1890

He is * { ~~Discharged~~ / Transferred to Army Reserve / ~~Disembodied~~ / ~~Demobilized~~ } on 4th February 1919
in consequence of **Demobilization.**

B. H. Grey Lieut .... Signature and Rank.

for Officer i/c MGCorps .... Records.

9.1 York St London .... (Place).

*Strike out whichever is inapplicable.
†The word "Nil" to be inserted when necessary.

GD1525 200,000 11/18 HWV(P1014)

Edward Rowbotham's demobilisation certificate listing him as medical category A1, no mean feat after three years in the trenches.

Above Left: Edward in uniform after demobilisation in 1919.

Above Right: Edward and Edie's wedding picture, 1920. *(Courtesy of Chris Hill)*

Below: Edward with his Home Guard unit, posing with a Vickers machine gun. Note that his uniform has a sergeant's three stripes. He was later told to remove one. Though a sergeant during the First World War, he was only allowed to be a corporal in the Home Guard, which he felt was a disgraceful insult.

Left: Edward in his Home Guard uniform wearing his First World War medals. His medals from left to right are the Military Medal, British War Medal and Victory Medal. He only wears the two stripes of a corporal.

Right: Edward and Edie Rowbotham with their daughter Edith in 1940.

Below: The surviving Rowbotham siblings in 1970. Top row: Edgar, Frank and Edward. Front row: Hilda and Ernest.

letter and I snatched up Albert's and read it quickly, so that I could take my time to savour the contents of Agnes's letter, which I expected to be full of the usual affection and cheerful titbits of news. But I was wrong. Agnes's letter was neither affectionate nor cheerful; she was breaking off our engagement. She concluded the cruelly brief note by asking if she should send the ring out to me or keep it till I came home. I was devastated and furious, and wrote back that I wanted her to send the ring to me immediately so that I could smash it into a thousand pieces. Of course, I had sensed that something wasn't quite right, but still, it came as a great shock to me. I felt at a very low ebb.

I had little time to brood, however, because a few days later, at the end of July 1917, we were plunged into the Third Battle of Ypres – one of the bloodiest of the war. This battle is sometimes known, for some reason, by the name of Passchendaele, although we were fighting much further to the south of that place. By the summer of 1917 the Flanders plain – after three years of pounding by shells – was just a sea of mud. The ground was pitted with filthy shell holes full of foul-smelling water (and worse), the trenches littered with unburied bodies stuck fast in the slime. To reach our positions, we had to stagger as best we could with our guns and equipment across duckboards; anyone falling off these duckboards was in genuine danger of drowning.

The trenches were not really trenches at all. They were breastworks (low temporary defences) built up on the boggy ground, using millions of sandbags in the zigzag shape of trenches. Duckboards were laid along the bottom for walking; even so, the water was often up to a foot deep. I remember the rain – we thought it would never stop – and the stinking, sticky mud. Everywhere there was mud and death.

The weather and the conditions we were fighting in were far more formidable enemies for us to overcome than the Jerries. Trying to go forward through the quagmire – with explosions occurring on every yard of ground; the smell of tear gas and gunpowder smoke; the stench of the putrefying bodies of men and mules all around us; and men falling everywhere, some only wounded then drowning as they were sucked into the mud – it was impossible not to be overwhelmed by the feeling that it was your turn next. At the end of each day, when it still hadn't happened, I offered up a silent prayer of thanksgiving. It is no wonder that in conditions like these men went mad. We were all affected in some way. The exhausted, hollow-eyed looks and drawn faces were characteristic of all of us to a greater or lesser degree.

When we eventually came out of the trenches for a brief respite and reorganisation, my section colleague, Corporal Barker, a Liverpool boy, noticed a difference in my demeanour, which he couldn't entirely put down to battle fatigue, and was a bit puzzled. He said so and asked me why. I told him I was all right and tried to make light of it, but I knew I really was a little down in spirit because of my broken engagement. I hadn't realised that it showed, but it evidently did. Corporal Barker, a good comrade and friend, was concerned about me and took steps to find out my fiancée's address. He must have talked to Lieutenant Van Someren about it, as Van Someren knew the addresses of all the correspondents of his men, as it was his job to censor all out-going letters, and possibly having read my angry letter to Agnes would have guessed what the trouble was. Corporal Barker wrote to Agnes — what he said I do not know — and he showed me the letter he received from Agnes in reply. In it, she thanked him for trying to put things right between us, but there was nothing he could do as 'Ted has said some unforgivable things in his last letter'. So, it was all my fault, apparently. And that was the end of my association with Miss Agnes Poyntz, the love of my life. The bleak and utterly devastated landscape of the battlefield seemed almost symbolic of my state of mind at that low point in my time in the British Army.

CHAPTER NINE

THE BATTLE OF CAMBRAI

Life in Flanders and Northern France was not quite all mud and blood, although it often seemed like it. We did have periodic 'rests' when we would leave the trenches. The rests were principally designed to get the men physically fit once more for the next operation. In the daytime, we would have training which consisted of drills, work on the guns and military exercises and manoeuvres. In the evenings we often had concerts, or occasionally we would be entertained by artistes from home. This was a morale-boosting exercise, and it worked for me. I really enjoyed these concerts; at such times, it was not only a relief to be away from the threat of imminent death, it felt great to be alive. We used to sing a song called 'Oh, oh, oh, it's a loverly war!' which went as follows:

Up to your waist in water. Up to your eyes in slush,
Who is more contented in all the world than us?
Oh, it's a cushy life, boys, really we love it so,
Once a fellow was sent on leave and simply refused to go!

Oh, oh, oh, it's a loverly war!
What do you want with eggs and ham
When you've got plum and apple jam?
Form fours! Right turn!

How do you spend the money you earn?
Oh, oh, oh, it's a loverly war!

There are many more verses, but the above is about all I can remember, which is probably just as well, as soldiers' songs in wartime were not particularly 'delicate'.

It was during one of these rests after the Third Battle of Ypres that boxing tournaments were introduced. These were designed to keep up the fighting spirit of the troops, as the morale of the Army was causing some anxiety in the High Command. Even we noticed that there was a certain lack of discipline and some disregard for rank.

The boxing tournaments were organised by the officers, and men were matched according to rank and the officers' judgment. Privates fought privates, lance corporals fought lance corporals, and so on. Personally, I was not particularly keen and was hoping I would not be matched with anyone; I had no interest in being thumped myself, or indeed thumping anyone else, for the amusement of the officers. However, I reckoned that if I was picked then I could call upon my pal, Garnet Davies, who was a professional boxer, to take me in hand and give me a few lessons in self-defence.

We had sparred together many times and he had told me I was coming along nicely, but that I shouldn't get too cocky – which I suppose I was. I thought I was hitting Garn when and where I liked, not realising, of course, that it was only by his permission. One day, when we had been sparring as usual and I was landing punches on him, he suddenly stopped me in my tracks with what seemed like a sledgehammer in my ribs. I was sure he had broken a rib. I said to him, 'What did you go and hit me that hard for, you bloody great bully?'

'That was only a flick,' he said. He had a grin on his face like a goat in a cabbage garden. Then he became serious and told me that although I was coming along all right I was not paying enough attention to defence and that an opponent could easily take advantage of that and almost certainly knock me out. 'I was doing you a favour, Ted.' He was right of course but it just didn't feel like it at that time.

The daily bouts continued, and I was not called upon to take part. By this time, the officers had managed to take over a deserted theatre and they'd rigged up a ring in the centre of the floor. It looked almost like a genuine boxing ring, raised about four feet from the ground, with room enough around it for all the spectators to sit down. I thought I had escaped been picked somehow, until one day, much to my regret, I heard that I had been 'matched' with a Corporal Dingwall. We were much the same weight and build. I was pleased to discover that he was no more keen about our fight than I was, so we discussed it and decided that there was no reason why we should knock each other about just for other people's amusement. We agreed to take things quietly, only tap each other lightly, and neither of us would deliver a damaging punch.

There was a noisy and enthusiastic audience on the night of two or three hundred or so, with the officers occupying the ring-side seats. There were several bouts before ours, and we waited nervously, stripped down to our boxing rig of singlet, trousers, socks and boxing gloves. I was thinking, 'I'll be glad when it's all over.' It was almost as nerve-racking as waiting for the whistle to go over the top.

Eventually – it seemed like hours – the announcement came: 'The next bout at about ten stone is, on my right, Corporal Dingwall of No. 1 Section, and on my left, Corporal Rowbotham of No. 2 Section. The referee is Company Sergeant Major Killoran.'

I remember thinking what a good name he had for a CSM, as he called us to the centre of the ring and gave us the usual instructions: to break cleanly and may the best man win etc. I recall glancing over at Garn Davies who was in my corner, and blissfully unaware of the arrangements my opponent and I had made. Then the bell went, and we approached each other and began to spar, just tapping each other lightly and doing a lot of dancing about. All was going according to plan, when about midway through the first round he gave me such a wallop that I was brought down for a count of six. Fortunately, the rounds were only two minutes long and I managed to weather the remainder of the round.

In my corner, Davies was a bit disappointed in me and told me to cut out the fancy stuff and get stuck in. I didn't need his advice, because

I was livid that Dingwall had gone back on our arrangement, I had already planned to go into the next round in a different frame of mind entirely.

In round two, every punch was delivered in earnest. He tried to nail me again and again, but the tuition I had received from Davies stood me in good stead and I managed to get in a few punches myself. It was a ding-dong round, and towards the end of it I caught him a beauty, flush on the jaw. He went staggering backwards right across the ring, and only saved himself from going through the ropes by flinging out his arms and grabbing hold of the top rope. He came to a halt finally, with his arms outstretched along the top rope, sitting on the lower one. I knew he was in a vulnerable position, being not actually down, but I decided not to follow up my advantage as he seemed quite unable to extricate himself from his ungainly position, and I could not bring myself to hit him where he was, although I was entitled to do so. I could hear the referee shouting at me to 'Fight on! Fight on!' and the crowd had started to shout too, 'Knock him out!' 'Knock him through the ropes!' But I still couldn't bring myself to hit him while he was on the ropes. Then I had an idea that I thought would keep everybody happy: I'd try to *pretend* to hit him.

Nobody was deceived. In fact, they soon started to laugh at my antics. Then, mercifully, the bell went. It signified the end of the round, and a reprieve, not only for Dingwall but for me too, for I could never have brought myself to strike a half-dazed man.

Back in my corner, Davies was pleased with my performance and urged me to follow it up in the next round and finish him off. I heard 'Seconds out! Round three!' and stood up ready to go on. Dingwall didn't stand up. His seconds announced that Dingwall was not continuing, and the referee came over to me and raised my hand in victory, amid great applause from the bloodthirsty crowd. That was my first and last appearance in a boxing ring – thank goodness.

The foregoing is typical of how our periodic rests were spent. We had some good times, comparatively speaking, and we made the most of them. However, one exercise which happened frequently during our rests I did not enjoy at all: that of being inoculated. It seemed to me that the medical staff were always at the ready with their syringes, and if we didn't get at least one jab for something or other every time we came out of the trenches, it certainly seemed like it to me. I hated the jabs as they always made me feel really ill.

After each inoculation we were excused duty for, if I remember rightly, 48 hours, and I needed every minute of it. There were many others like me of course, but there were some who never seemed to be adversely affected at all. Significantly, one of the latter was Garnet Davies who twice had trench fever and was eventually invalided home. This led me to the conclusion that the men who suffered most from the inoculations were the ones least affected by the diseases, for whatever perverse reason.

I do not suppose that the inoculations were all specifically against trench fever, but, at the time, we had no idea what they were for. As well as our infestations of lice (and the inoculations certainly didn't get rid of *them*), we must have been exposed to millions of other vicious germs and bugs, which would have thrived in the conditions of almost constant filth in which we had to live.

Another aspect of life on active service which I think is worthy of mention is the phenomenon of sleep. The ideal conditions for sleep are usually a tranquil atmosphere and a nice warm, comfortable bed, conditions which were not that easy to find on a battlefield! Nevertheless, the human body, especially an active youthful body, demands sleep whatever the conditions or the place.

Living in the trenches, the mind and body became so attuned to the conditions that, whenever the opportunity presented itself, men were able to will themselves to sleep, and for just the length of time they wanted to sleep, irrespective of any explosions or other events which were occurring around them. This may sound fantastic today, but it is perfectly true, as I know from personal experience. I will give two examples, although I could give similar ones many times over.

The first that comes to mind is of an occasion near Bapaume, on the Somme. It was the night I have already described, when we were preparing for an attack at dawn. In the newly-dug trenches there were no dugouts as yet. So, we hollowed out recesses for ourselves in the sides of the trench. The recesses were about eighteen inches deep, about a foot high and about six feet long – not exactly the Ritz, but, we had no difficulty at all going to sleep. We just rolled ourselves into the recesses and we were out like a light.

We became used to this type of 'bedroom', rolling into them for our brief off-duty spells to sleep, irrespective of shell-fire or anything else the Jerries might send over. They offered us little protection, but by then we had all become fatalistic; we knew that if a shell was going to hit our spot it would whether we were asleep or not. As the war progressed, old trenches collapsed under shell-fire and had to be re-dug, and dugouts became increasingly makeshift. But, in the absence of proper dugouts, and if we had no time to hollow out enough recesses, the only other alternative was to simply sleep standing up, leaning forward into the sloping trench wall. And yes, we could all go to sleep standing up too, although this hindered the passage of other men along the trench.

Another example of this ability we acquired to 'command' sleep was during our periods of rest, particularly if we were out of the trenches and were expecting to stay out for some time. Of course, sudden emergencies arose all the time, and these rests were often interrupted. Our Company would suddenly receive orders to return to the trenches as soon as possible, and we immediately had to start preparing to leave, getting guns, ammunition and personal equipment ready. As soon as we had finished our preparations, we would calculate how long we had until it was time to 'fall in' ready for moving off. If we were lucky, and the time allowed for one or perhaps two hours, we would use that time to sleep. We needed no alarm clock or bed; we could just lie down anywhere and wake up at exactly the right hour to 'fall in'. Would that I could still do it now, as often I lie awake half the night trying to go to sleep – one of the many penalties of old age, I suppose.

I suppose today people would call it a victory of 'mind over matter', but I think it shows the wonderful adaptability of the human animal to the circumstances in which he finds himself.

When we went back into the trenches after our rest following the Third Battle of Ypres, we were fortunate in that the sector we moved into contained good, deep trenches and proper dugouts to live in. We were in the second line of trenches, which were on high ground and dry for a change, with the front line below us about 100 yards ahead. So, we were in a position to fire over the heads of the front line troops if and when necessary. This position was comparatively comfortable and was fairly quiet, except for frequent night raids by one side or the other.

It was here that I received the grim news of my brother. Tom's ship, the SS *Kilmayo* had been sunk in enemy action in the Bristol Channel in May 1917, and all hands had been lost except for one, whose testimony confirmed the loss. The news shook me deeply, and my reaction was bitter. To think that my young brother, still only in his teens, should be killed by enemy action. At that moment, my hatred of the Germans was so intense that, on looking back now, I can scarcely believe I was capable of such hatred. I vowed to kill seven Germans for my brother's death. Why seven? I didn't know then and I don't know now, but that was the number that came into my mind as I vowed to avenge the death of Tom. Our position behind the front line and a series of other coincidences enabled me to fulfil my vow that very same night.

Orders came to us during the day that we were to lay (aim) the gun on the German front line and fire all night at infrequent intervals. The intervals of firing were not to be regular but varied so that the Germans could not take advantage of the lulls. I was in charge of the gun team and I announced to the boys that I intended to fire the gun myself all night long and I would need only one sentry at a time instead of the usual two. This meant that each man needed to do only one hour on sentry duty and five hours off, as there were six of them.

I carried out my intention and fired the machine gun at intervals throughout the night. When daylight came, we dismantled the gun for cleaning while the other boys boiled water for making tea. After breakfast, we were sitting in the trench taking things easy when along came a man of the Notts and Derby Regiment, who had come via the communication trench from the front line.

He asked, 'Is this the gun that's been firing all night?'

'Yes,' I said, 'Is anything wrong?'

'Far from it,' he replied. 'We've been out in front all night repairing the wire [barbed wire entanglements] and the Jerries have been trying to sneak forward, throwing hand grenades. They couldn't quite reach us, thanks to your gun. Now there are seven of 'em lying on their own wire.'

I should have been delighted with this news, but I was not. I found I gained no satisfaction from it whatsoever; in fact, I was overcome by a feeling of deep remorse. 'Revenge is sweet' as the saying goes, but not for me. This may sound daft coming from a soldier on the front line of a war, but for the first time I felt like a murderer. All day I could not stop thinking about those seven men; men I had killed in revenge for my brother. Those men probably had brothers too, who would be mourning them, just as I was mourning Tom, and I had created another seven sad families. From 50 years away I can still call to mind the intensity of my feelings that morning.

However, those were thoughts that I, as a soldier whose *job* it was to kill, could not afford to entertain for long, for the stark fact is that a soldier in war is there to kill or be killed. In retrospect I suppose I did a good job in killing those seven Germans, thus preventing them from killing perhaps many more of our Notts and Derby comrades. I think it was Robert Burns who said 'Man's inhumanity to Man makes countless thousands mourn.' How true that is. Old Rabbie knew what he was talking about.

We were not in that sector of the line for long. We soon moved further south once more to take over part of the French line. There was nothing remarkable about this except that the French officer whom we were relieving could not speak English and our officer, who was taking over from him, could not speak French. Unfortunately, when taking over a new position, it was absolutely vital that the incoming unit should know all there was to know about the terrain, the enemy dispositions, and so on. So these two officers were in a quandary. Each of them had asked if there were any linguists among their own men, but had drawn a blank. German, Spanish and Italian were all mentioned but none of these were common to the two officers. Then one of them suggested Portuguese, and bingo! They could both speak a little Portuguese. So, the handing over of position was carried out in Portuguese. It would have been hilarious if there hadn't been a war on.

Of course, no-one knew what was going on at the time, but there had been a mutiny in the French Army. We did not find out any of the details until a year after it had been quelled. It was not until recently that I learned the full story of the French Mutiny when I was reading some books on the First World War. Apparently, mutinies occurred in sixteen different army corps, with some French infantrymen marching through the streets of a town baa-ing like sheep, to indicate they were being driven like lambs to the slaughter. The ringleaders were all executed and the men went back to war. Miraculously, the Germans never got an inkling of it until it was too late. It seems there was as much inefficiency behind the German lines as behind the French and ours.

At this time – the autumn of 1917, the morale of the British Army was not high either, as evidenced by the slackness in saluting officers when out of the line, and the ignoring of the National Anthem at the end of concerts and the like. It never sank to the level of mutiny, however.

So, after our brief 'respite' our Company marched south again to fight the Battle of Cambrai. The Battle of Cambrai was heralded as such a great victory that church bells were rung in England for the first time in the war, although there was still massive loss of life. This was the first time that most of us had fought in open country, and having penetrated the Hindenburg Line and advanced something like four or five miles, we thought, in our ignorance, that the war couldn't possibly last for much longer.

The Battle of Cambrai commenced on 20 November 1917, with many tanks and without the usual preliminary bombardment, so the last few hours and minutes before going over the top were much easier on our nerves, especially as we were not to be first to encounter the enemy. Hundreds of tanks were to go first and we were to follow them. As we reached our objectives we would stop temporarily to allow a following unit to 'pass through' us and continue while our particular 'wave' would consolidate the positions we had captured. This attack must have been a complete surprise to the enemy, and we captured thousands of prisoners – I believe about 7,000 – and lots of 'material' such as guns. The 'material' we were most interested in however, were the provisions. I remember quite a number of loaves of black bread which we had heard about but had not seen before. The unappetising reports about it had not been exaggerated. Though it looked quite good with its brown-black crust, it was heavy and doughy and had a sour taste.

As we had almost forgotten what real white bread tasted like, we ate it anyway, in preference to our hard biscuits only for the reason that we could satisfy our hunger more quickly. It was far from being the quality of our own or French bread. The loaves were shaped similar to bricks, except that they were somewhat longer and about four or five inches square. Sadly, apart from bread, the Germans had left little else in the way of food and soon it was back to our biscuits and bully beef.

After we had maintained a position for a little while, we moved on to a new position, leap-frogging through other troops in the planned tactical manner. By the end of that first day, we had advanced several miles and found ourselves in trenches that were still being constructed. Instead of digging dugouts, we each made our own recess in the wall of the trench; that was where we rested and did our cooking, such as it was.

Our positions were at the head of the thrust towards Cambrai, and the Germans were very quiet. Our greatest enemy was the cold at night. The winter weather was bad enough in the daytime, but at night it was intense, and seemed worse because we had no proper shelter and could not move about in the trenches to keep our blood circulating.

One night in particular was very cold indeed. It was the kind of bitter cold that almost stops your breath. Lying in my fox-hole, I thought there was a real possibility I could actually freeze to death. I had an idea and made a little pigeonhole in the back of my recess, into which I put a lighted candle. Then I pulled my greatcoat tightly around me and lay down with my back towards the candle, taking care not to let my back touch the candle itself. Well, I must have fallen asleep, for soon afterwards I became aware of a surge of warmth and realised at once that I was on fire. Even so, I didn't move for several seconds. The warmth was so delicious, it was only very reluctantly I got out of my hole to put myself out. I had to rub my back up against the sides of the trench a few times before I was properly 'out'. I was lucky: I was not burnt in any way, as my clothing seemed to have smouldered rather than burst into flames.

For this folly, I paid dearly. A hole at least four inches across was burnt right through my greatcoat and every layer of clothing to my bare skin. The wind blowing around my midriff was anything but pleasant. But, what cannot be cured must be endured, so they say, and so it was until we came out of the trenches, which was not to be for several very cold and draughty weeks, as on 30 November 1917, the Germans launched their counter-attack.

They attacked on both flanks in an attempt to encircle the forward divisions. It nearly succeeded – but not quite. They succeeded to the extent that all the forward troops had to retire pretty sharpish to defensive positions, in the process giving up nearly all the ground we had just won. We held the positions until we were relieved on 23 December, two days before Christmas. We had been fighting, unrelieved, for nearly five weeks. During this time, none of us had been able to have as much as a wash or a shave – my beard could have rivalled Rip Van Winkle's.

An amusing story comes out of this. We had been in close proximity to the Notts and Derbys all this time and we had got to know each other very well. There was one young Notts man whose face was smooth except for a little soft down – I had talked to this man many times during our time in Cambrai and got to know him quite well.

When we came out of the trenches, we were stationed in a small village. As soon as we arrived, everyone at once became busy getting rid of their unwanted beards and lice, and having a good wash and change of clothing. Afterwards, some of us went off to explore the village. We found the inevitable estaminet and went in. There, against the bar, stood our friend of the smooth face. He showed no sign of recognition when I said, 'How's things, mate?'

He looked very puzzled as he answered, 'All right, thanks.' Then he said, 'Where have I seen you before? I know the voice but can't place you.'

It was hardly surprising really; the last time we had spoken, I was wearing a steel helmet, and my grime-encrusted face had sported a wild and hairy beard, and now I was washed, clean-shaven and wearing my ordinary military cap.

'So, you can't place me, eh?' I said to him. 'I've only been in the trenches with you for the past five weeks!'

I could see it dawning on him. He started laughing and said he would never have recognised me, as without the beard I looked at least ten years younger. I suppose I should have been flattered.

Our billets were in a large barn where there were 'bunks' of wire netting and wooden frames for us to sleep in. There was also a good sized brazier with an enormous fire of charcoal and coke burning in the centre of the barn. It was lovely and warm, and to complete our feelings of luxury, there was a plentiful supply of food, including fresh bread. After so many weeks of privations, not to mention a great big hole in my coat, this seemed like the best hotel in the world.

In 'idyllic' conditions such as this, there always has to be a Jonah. It was Christmas Eve and all of us who were not on duty had made plans for the evening. My plan, with five or six others, was to go to the estaminet and have a few drinks. The Jonah? Yes, he arrived in the person of a certain Corporal Musson. He had been away from the Company for some time (possibly injured, I don't remember) and had not been in action with us in Cambrai. He was a good soldier, but had an unfortunate, dour and unpleasant personality. He was a member of our original Company, so everyone knew him and greeted him accordingly. My own greeting to him, as a fellow Corporal was, 'How are you, Muss?'

'All right,' he said in a surly voice and manner which seemed to suggest that he was *not* all right.

I thought little of it, however, until just after tea-time, when we were getting 'poshed up' for our evening out, in the Christmas spirit, most of us whistling or humming a tune. I noticed Musson was not getting ready, but sitting on his own by the brazier, with his hands dangling over his knees. I wondered if perhaps he didn't have any money, so I went over to him and said, 'Aren't you going out, Muss? If you're short of money, I can lend you some.' Not that I was all that flush, but I wouldn't see a comrade broke, especially on Christmas Eve.

'No, I'm not broke,' he answered. 'And it's my business whether I go out or not.'

'Good enough,' I said and left him to his sweet thoughts.

Just before we went out, I overheard Musson muttering to himself. He was saying something about somebody going to be sorry before the night was out. I believe I was meant to overhear it. Others said that he seemed to be breathing hate, and he had threatened someone. On the walk into the village, we speculated as to who might be Musson's intended victim, but I had already come to the conclusion that it was probably me. Musson had it in for me. I never knew why; I never had that much to do with the fellow, much less having ever been in a position to antagonise him. Anyway, whoever his grudge was against, he obviously did not have the courage to come out with it while everyone was sober. His plan was evidently to wait until his victim was well-oiled and unable to defend himself. Having made up my mind that it was I who was to be his punch-bag, I decided that not one drop of alcohol would pass my lips that evening.

My suspicions were confirmed during the evening, as the boys' tongues became looser as the evening wore on. They were sure that I was 'the one'. So, my first evening off, after all the miseries and deprivations of the past weeks was being wrecked by a moron, and I was feeling anything but Christmas goodwill towards Corporal Musson.

When we got back to the billet, he was still in the same position as when we left. I went straight up to him and said, 'Here I am, Musson.

Now let's see what you're made of. You've spoilt my night out, so come outside and carry out those threats you've been making about someone being sorry.'

He could see I was not drunk as he had expected, and protested that he did not mean me.

'Well, who *did* you mean, then?' I demanded.

His explanation was not very convincing, but he obviously didn't want a showdown, and by now the boys were trying to get me to let it drop. Any of my past or present acquaintances could vouchsafe the fact that, by nature, I am not a quarrelsome person, but if I feel that I am being unjustly treated or maligned I will not hesitate to stand up for myself. So, to round off our argument, I told Musson that if he felt like taking a rise out of me at any time then to do it openly and I would oblige him. Little did I know just how soon he was to get the chance to 'nobble' me.

The next day was Christmas. We were out of the line with plenty to eat and drink and little to do after church parade. Soon after tea, my old friend Garnet Davies, who was now Sergeant Davies, came to my billet to say he had obtained permission for me to spend the evening with him in the sergeants' mess. This was grand, as we had not spent much time together over the last few months and had much to talk about. We had a glorious binge, and we both got very sozzled. While it scarcely showed with Davies, it certainly did with me: I was as drunk as the proverbial lord. I would go as far as to say that in all my life, before or since that occasion, I have never been so drunk. My legs would not function properly, and Davies had to almost carry me up the road to my billet, which was about 100 yards away.

As we arrived, I remember shouting to Musson, 'Now's your chance, Muss. I'm drunk tonight. Just what you wanted, ain't it?' Davies was trying to shut me up as he rolled me into my bunk and told me to get to sleep.

I quite expected Musson to attack me in my sleep, but I didn't care; the booze had made me impervious to fear of him, and I must have fallen asleep immediately. I didn't know at the time, but Davies had gone over to speak to Musson before he left me, and threatened him that if he so much as laid a finger on me while I was in such a state he would kill him. So, why had Musson taken against me so? I had no idea then and I have no idea now. I suppose the war did funny things to people.

I remember this incident very clearly, despite the amount I'd had to drink. I would like to make a point here, and it is a view I have held for a very long time. Many times I have spoken to men who say they do not remember anything of their misdeeds or pranks of the 'night before', when they have been drunk, but I remember the above episode as though it happened last week. I have always had a very retentive memory, so it may be that people with a less retentive memory really do forget what they do. However, it has never happened to me; not that I have ever been an habitual boozer, but I suppose in my life there have been many special occasions when I have had one or two over the eight. At this time in my life, though, I seldom touch strong drink.

Now that I have well and truly polished up my halo, I will move on to the next chapter.

CHAPTER TEN

PROMOTED TO SERGEANT – DEATH OF PRIVATE CHATWIN

Christmas Day was over and Boxing Day arrived, together with my terrible hangover. I felt awful as we trooped out, under Lieutenant Van Someren, to do revolver practice. The Army would have done better to have saved the ammunition, for the results were shocking, as I was not the only soldier that day to be suffering with a hangover. Van Someren himself was not brilliant, but he put up a better show than I did. Most of our Section were usually good shots, but on this occasion the standard fell very badly and everyone was glad when the session was over, including Van Someren, who had obviously had a good time the previous night too.

A few days later, we were on the march again to yet another part of the line, but before we went to the firing line, we halted for several days to make up 'wastage' of men and material. It was during this pause that I was promoted to sergeant. Now I was level with my best pal, Davies, who had always been one stripe ahead of me. He was delighted and remarked that he would no longer have to ask permission for me to join him in the sergeants' mess. For the remaining few days preceding our move to the line I had my meals in the sergeants' mess and felt a little embarrassed, but also proud, in my brand new stripes, and enjoyed the banter with the other sergeants. I was also looking forward to Davies' company during our periods of rest from the trenches, but

I was due for a disappointment: during the next spell on the front line, Davies was struck for the second time with trench fever and was sent back home to Blighty.

I never set eyes on my pal again. Some years after the war, I did make an attempt to get back in touch with him. As I have stated before, he lived in the Lye near Stourbridge. It was about 1934 and I had a job driving a delivery van and making deliveries around Cradley, Dudley, Oldbury and Birmingham. One day I was sent to Stourbridge and on the way passed through the Lye. The name immediately reminded me that this was the place where my old comrade had lived and I decided to make some enquiries about him.

It was lunchtime and I spotted some workmen going into a pub and I thought that surely one of them would know him. So, I went in and called for a half pint and asked the workmen who were standing at the bar if they knew a Garnet Davies. I explained that we had been old comrades in the war and I wanted to look him up. One of the men did indeed know him.

'He had trench fever,' the man said, 'and was sent home. He's got a son about seventeen or eighteen and does a bit of boxing?'

'Yes, that's him!' I replied. The son would have been the baby who was born while Garnet was on active service with me around 1916–17. I had found my old mate!

I was about to ask if the man knew Davies's address but he added, 'If you're thinking of going to see him mate, I should forget it. He's mad! He knocks his wife about and goes off with other women. He doesn't work, *won't* work, and is always in trouble with the police.'

I could not believe we were talking about the same man; Garn had been the best comrade a soldier ever had. I told the man that when I had known Garnet Davies he was very fond of his wife and would never have looked at another woman, he was sober-minded and never disagreeable or violent.

'That was before the war, mate,' said the man. 'He was never the same after. They say the trench fever affected his mind as well as his body. If you take my tip, you'll leave him be.'

I thanked the man, drank up and left, feeling disappointed and very sorry for my old comrade, with whom I had shared some terrible ordeals. I felt something of a traitor in deciding not to go and see him, but if I had called on him, I would have been obliged to observe the convention of the time and invite him back to my home – and I considered that my first duty was to my wife and child (our daughter was thirteen at that time). So, I let it lie.

The incident troubled me. I entertained some strange thoughts that day on my way home. I wondered how many more men there were like Davies, who had served their country bravely and should have come back as heroes but came back ruined. The Great War was still claiming casualties long after the Armistice was signed.

Back to January 1918. After about a week, we went 'up the line' again – we were somewhere on the Somme – half the Company in and the other half out, which was the usual procedure when no actual battles were in progress. This procedure, of course, applied to the whole Battalion (32 machine guns in all) and provided machine-gun cover for the whole of the 6th Division. Thus we covered a fairly extensive front. I mention this fact because, with these interchanging positions, which spread the burden so to speak, we were likely to be sent anywhere along the Divisional front. Some positions were cushy, whilst others were less so, which was probably the reason for our frequent interchanges.

One particular position I have in mind was a 'secret' position, the terrain low-lying, with boggy ground between us and the enemy, who were entrenched in some higher ground beyond the bog, whilst we were on higher ground on our side of the bog. Our front line was some 200 yards in front of our position, and we could fire over the heads of our troops ahead of us if necessary. Our dugout was built into a fairly large hillock and provided plenty of room for the seven of us. The gun emplacement was situated on top and well camouflaged.

Inside the dugout, a well timbered, square tunnel went into the hillside for a distance of about six yards and provided good sleeping quarters for four men. All in all, it was the best dugout we had occupied for a very long time – almost five star! It had one snag, however. The doorway, which was covered by a large camouflaged blanket, faced the enemy lines. This meant we could not move outside during daylight hours.

What had once been a road leading to a nearby village, but now not much more than a footpath, ran outside our 'front door'. We had a good view of the enemy lines by looking through a slit in the blanket, but we had to be very careful not to disturb the blanket, for if we had been spotted we had no protection. The Jerries would have been able to put a shell right into our living quarters.

It was winter, early February 1918, and every morning a mist lay in the low-lying ground between the lines, and this gave us an opportunity to explore our immediate surroundings for about an hour or so each day until the mist dissipated. Just outside the village, which had been ruined by shell-fire, we discovered a small cemetery, which seemed to have taken the brunt of the shells. It was no more than 50 yards long by about 20 yards wide, but it provided one of the strangest sights I encountered in the whole of the war. At one end of the cemetery was an enormous cross, a life-sized crucifix, absolutely undamaged except for one small bullet hole in the leg of the figure of Jesus. At the other end of the cemetery was one solitary grave, the only one in the cemetery that had not been destroyed by shells. We could scarcely believe our eyes. The grave itself was surrounded by a scrolled, wrought iron fence about a foot or so high, while at the head of the grave was a headstone also made of wrought iron, in the centre of which was a brass plate bearing the name, age and other particulars of the deceased. As far as we could translate, the grave contained the body of an eighteen-year-old girl whose first name was Marie.

What surprised us more than anything else was to find intact one of those Victorian flower containers: it had a black wooden base on which artificial flowers were mounted and then covered by a glass dome. To find all this, especially glass, untouched on one solitary grave, surrounded as it was by such devastation, seemed miraculous. The only damage appeared to be that the glass dome was tilted a little and the inside of the glass had become dirty. I picked up the glass and cleaned it while the other boys wiped the dirt off the flowers. Then we carefully replaced it, paid our respects to the grave and went on our way. Whilst it was very unusual to have found a grave so remarkably untouched, it was actually not an uncommon sight to come upon a crucifix or a wayside shrine intact in the midst of utter destruction; so much so that I believe the phenomenon has been commented upon by others both during and since the war.

Back in our dugout before the morning mist cleared, we began to make tea and prepare breakfast, our rations having being brought to us overnight. The conversation over breakfast was monopolised by what we had seen at the cemetery. The three who had not been with us were inclined to be a little sceptical; they could believe that the cross and even a grave might somehow survive undamaged, but for something made of glass to have survived the constant, pounding shell-fire seemed unimaginable. So, I promised to show them the next morning.

We passed the day sleeping, eating and talking, while one man at a time took his turn on duty, taking a frequent look through the blanket at what was happening in the enemy lines. When it was sufficiently dark to emerge from the dugout, we all went out to the gun emplacement, removed the camouflage, and checked the gun and ammunition. We would remain outside as long as we could to enjoy the fresh air after being cooped up all day in the dugout. After a while, the winter chill would force us back inside the dugout, leaving just the two sentries on lookout.

That particular night, I remember, I decided to have a lie down in the tunnel, as it was more comfortable than sitting in the dugout. Lying there with my thoughts, I was aware of some desultory shelling going on in the vicinity of the village, but it was not sufficiently close to cause any concern to us. As I lay there quietly thinking, I felt myself dozing off, and had reached that half-way state between consciousness and sleep, when a remarkable thing happened. Suddenly, I realised that although I was still lying down I was not in the tunnel. Space and time seemed to have 'slipped' slightly and there was sky above me, not dark anymore but a beautiful clear blue. From above there came an apparition which hovered a few feet above me. It was the figure of a young girl in white, flowing robes – an angel. The face, which I saw quite clearly, was beautiful, and bore an expression of such compassion, that I find it hard to put it adequately into words.

She extended her arms towards me as though to embrace me. I wanted to raise my arms to receive the embrace, but as soon as I tried to tell my brain to move the first muscle, everything vanished and I was back again lying in the tunnel. I lay still for some time afterwards, waiting, hoping for the beautiful vision to reappear, but sadly it did not come.

This whole experience could not have lasted many seconds, but it has remained engraved on my memory as the most beautiful moment of my life. It was not a physical experience but purely spiritual, with not the slightest inference of love or sex: it transcended all earthly emotions. I realise, of course, that some doubt may be entertained of the truth of this story, but no amount of doubt would affect my knowledge of it. There is that old Shakespeare line that there are 'more things in heaven and earth than are dreamt of in our philosophy'. He was referring to the supernatural, and I believe that what happened to me in that tunnel was a manifestation beyond our normal understanding: I truly believed I had been visited by an angel.

The next morning was again misty, and I took the three men with me who had doubted what we had seen the previous day. I wanted them to see for themselves the sight which had left such an impression on the rest of us. As we approached the little cemetery, however, I realised that it was not to be. The crucifix was still untouched, but, on the spot where the intact grave had been the day before, there was now a huge shell crater. It had received a direct hit. There was not a sign of either the glass dome of flowers or the wrought iron fencing and headstone. Nothing remained at all. I searched about but could find not a single trace of the young girl's grave; it had been blown to smithereens.

We all looked into the great gaping hole. It was obvious that the shell crater was new, and the fact that I had led my mates straight to that particular spot went some way to convince them of the truth of our story, especially as the crucifix was still intact. I told the others of the 'vision' I had experienced in the tunnel the night before. You might think they would have laughed at me, as grown men discussing 'visions' would seem a little fantastic in everyday life, but they took it very seriously. This was, of course, far from everyday life: we were living, eating, sleeping and fighting in an atmosphere where death was always looking over the shoulders of men and we saw strange and miraculous things happen every day. One asked me if I had been scared, but I replied that it hadn't been frightening at all, but a wonderful experience. Another suggested that the 'angel' was the soul of the young girl whose grave had been destroyed, that she had come to thank us for cleaning up her grave and paying our respects. I would like to think that was the correct explanation for what happened to me that night.

It was in the same dugout that a more humorous incident occurred. Never before had we received fresh meat in the line, but for some reason unknown to us, we started receiving plentiful supplies of mutton chops night after night in our rations. There was still no proper bread, though, just the usual hard tack biscuits. So, not having bread to soak up the mutton fat, everything we had that would hold fat was filled with it, as we could not bring ourselves to throw it away; after all, it was food, but what to do with it was the problem. We discussed it among ourselves and decided we could make some sort of pudding – but none of us had the slightest idea how to do it. So, one bright spark piped up, 'Why don't you have a bash at it, Sarge?'

It appeared no-one else wanted the job, so reluctantly I agreed. I looked around for inspiration. We had a good supply of biscuits, and I set the men to pounding them to pieces, eventually reducing them to something resembling very coarse oatmeal. I have no idea what the biscuits were actually made of, but they resembled large dog biscuits. Anyway, the resulting 'oatmeal' was put to soak in water for a while to soften it without making it too sloppy. Then I melted the mutton fat, and, perhaps rather tardily, I washed my hands before scooping the meal into an improvised mixing bowl. I poured the melted mutton fat over it and began to mix, first with a spoon and then with my hands until the 'pastry' was manageable, then formed it into three balls, two of them about five inches across and the third a little larger than a tennis ball. I then hollowed them out with my hands and put jam – the ubiquitous plum and apple – in the centres then sealed them. We happened to have a few new sandbags, which were the cleanest material we had, and we cut three squares out of one of them and wrapped the puddings in them, tying them tightly at the top (which, we later discovered, was a mistake, as it did not allow for swelling). We thought they looked something like a pawnbroker's sign when tied onto a stick and suspended in a petrol can with the top removed, containing about three inches of water to steam them. We made a charcoal fire and let them steam for about two hours, then we set to, everyone eager to see what my 'recipe' tasted like. Well, even if I say so myself, it tasted delicious. But, oh, the weight of it! We could feel it going down like lumps of lead, but it tasted so good and different after our diet of bully beef and biscuits that we ate the lot. It certainly filled us up and it was sometime before we felt hungry again. No-one thought to compliment the 'chef'; on the contrary, someone said it was just as well we hadn't got to go 'over the top' that day because we would never make it up the sides of the trench – such ingratitude!

Incidentally, the improvised mixing bowl was a child's enamel totty pot, liberated from the nearby village. Let me add though, that the totty pot had been used for a long time by us as a wash basin and shaving mug, and we had thoroughly cleaned it with sand and water beforehand to make it 'hygienic'.

Soon after this, in accordance with the interchanging system, we found ourselves in another part of the Divisional sector and things were quiet, ominously quiet, all along the front, and it was there that another link in the chain of my apparently charmed life was forged.

It was 18 March 1918 (you will soon realise why I remember the date so clearly), and when the ration party came up that night they brought a message for the next one of my team due home-leave to go back with them to Company HQ. They also brought a list of the names of towns in England where there was an epidemic of a fever raging. I believe we were told it was scarlet fever, but it might have been the start of Spanish Influenza. Men whose homes were in those towns could not go there on leave, but if they wished, they could go to another town. It so happened that the next man due leave, whose name was Richards, lived in one of the towns where the fever raged. It also happened that my name, Rowbotham, was next on the list, and there was no report of the fever in my home town.

Richards was in a quandary, whether to go somewhere else or wait until the epidemic was over. He chose to wait. I, even though I had most to gain, tried to persuade him to go somewhere else – I really did – having in mind that my own leave would be only ten days away and we were on a quiet front (but little did I know what was soon to happen). But Richards declined, so I took his place and went back with the ration party and crossed the Channel for home on 20 March.

On 21 March, all hell broke loose. The Germans, under General von Ludendorff, launched a great offensive that morning with almost unprecedented ferocity; history later recorded that over three million shells were fired by the Germans in the first three hours of bombardment, and over 38,000 British troops were put out of action that day, over 20,000 of them taken prisoner by the Jerries. It became known as the Second Battle of the Somme, and my mates were slap-bang in the middle of it. Our Company was virtually wiped out; when my leave-companion and I returned, we recognised only six men of the 130 we had left less than two weeks earlier. There were one or two officers spared, but I was very sad to learn that Lieutenant Van Someren had been killed. Van Someren had conducted himself very bravely by all accounts, but had fallen at the end of the first day. Another who did not survive was the man whose place I had taken to go on leave, Richards.

Needless to say, the enjoyment of my leave had been marred by this sudden offensive. Back in England I was reading the newspaper reports, and knew exactly where the fighting was taking place, and knew that my comrades were in the thick of it. Not that I felt heroic and wished that I had been with them – I wasn't that daft! I could only be thankful that I had been extremely lucky not to have been caught up in that particular slaughter.

It could not fail to cast a shadow over what should have been an enjoyable homecoming and welcome respite from life in the trenches. I tried to dismiss it from my mind, because there was nothing at all I could do about it, but I often wondered how the boys were faring, and of course, I knew that I would be in it myself before long. My family and friends were very good at distracting me though, and I needed them more than ever because this was my first leave without Agnes. While I had become accustomed to our estrangement while in France, it was a little different when I came home, and I could not help but compare my last leave with this one.

During this leave, I met my prospective brother-in-law, an Australian corporal by the name of Percival Eagleton, who was paying court to my youngest sister, Nellie. We got on well together. He was a man of forceful personality and charm, the sort of person who managed to get his own way in most things, and we enjoyed discussing the merits and demerits of our two armies, the British and the Australian. I discovered among other things that Percy, as a corporal in the Australian Army, was receiving seven shillings and sixpence a day, while I, a sergeant in the British Army, received only three shillings a day, which didn't exactly please me much.

My sister was about twenty years of age at this time. She was lovely and as pretty as a picture – no wonder he fell in love with her. They were talking of an early marriage and I tried to persuade Nellie to wait until the war was over, but I should have saved my breath as they were married soon afterwards. So much for brotherly influence!

Among the friends I met during my ten days' leave were Phoebe and Harry Collingswood, who kept an off-licence two doors away, in Church Street, Bloxwich. In conversation, I asked Phoebe how her sister, Lily, was getting on (Lily had been one of my teenage 'flames'). She told me she was working in a hotel in Birmingham, but was coming over the next weekend. Unfortunately, I had to be back in France before then, so I gave Phoebe my address and asked her to give it to Lily with a request that she would write to me. It was heart-warming to receive a week or so later, when I was back in France, a lovely long letter from Lily. From then on, we kept up a regular correspondence right up to the end of the war. What happened then I will come to later.

Back in France, I was dismayed to find that my Company had been almost completely wiped out. The powers-that-be had moved quickly and had already reinforced our Company to fighting strength again. The 71st Company had now become part of the 6th Machine Gun Battalion; my Company had become C Company. We had only a few days to coordinate ourselves before joining the battle in an endeavour to check the German onslaught, which they had managed to sustain since 21 March. The offensive was eventually checked, but with terrific losses on both sides.

New faces! New faces! That is what I remember of that time. New faces all the time to replace the casualties. No sooner did we get used to the new faces than they would be replaced by others, which gives some indication of the scale of our losses. New officers gave orders to new men. New men obeyed those orders as efficiently as if they had always been with that same officer; it had to be done, because training in machine-gunnery *had* to be efficient or it was useless. But the 'personal touch' was lacking. We had no time to get to know the men we were fighting alongside, but we carried on just the same, trying our best with new friends, losing old ones – and all to satisfy the appetite of the insatiable war machine. And, in this war, it had become more than clear to us that men were expendable.

The German offensive continued, with varying intensity, until the end of April. The Jerries had broken through the British lines and we were in retreat. Nothing was worse for morale than fighting continuous rearguard actions with your comrades in retreat. It gave us a feeling of inferiority, especially when we knew we were outnumbered by three or four to one. The Germans seemed to be unstoppable, their men reinforced by troops released from the Russian front following the collapse of the Russians the previous year. We counter-attacked many times and regained some ground, but each time we had to give way again under their overwhelming weight of numbers, not to say their use of every fiendish device they could muster, such as gas shells (which contained mustard gas), tear gas, mortars, machine guns, and high explosive shells ranging in calibre from three inches to fifteen-inch naval shells. They also used a missile, which we named the 'flying pig', which we could see coming through the air (much bigger than the dreaded *minenwerfer* trench mortar), and when it exploded, it shook the ground like an earth tremor.

I learned later that the Germans had relied on their 'new' mustard gas to penetrate the British gas masks and kill us off without resistance, but fortunately for us, our gas masks stood up to it, uncomfortable though they were when we had to wear them for long periods. These 'box respirators' as they were called were a considerable improvement on the old hood respirators, and we were thankful to the boffins who invented it, for it saved many thousands of lives.

Towards the end of April 1918, the German onslaught had finally been brought to a halt, with massive losses on both sides, but the German losses had been greater; we had watched German troops being mown down like grass before scythes by our machine guns.

The front line became more or less static, with just intermittent artillery and machine-gun fire, and some night raids and general air activity during the days. It was quiet once more after the monstrous, relentless shelling, which we had had to endure for weeks on end. The noise of the shelling sent men mad. It was far more than just noise; the ceaseless pounding shook not only your body, and deafened your ears, it seemed to get inside your head. No wonder men went insane. A new name had been invented to describe this madness: they called it shell shock. Shell shock caused some men to shake and tremble or become incoherent, others to become withdrawn and morose. At its worst it would make men go berserk and was terrible to see. Even after the war not everyone recovered.

This quiet period gave me a chance to take things easy and do a little letter writing. During moments like these, you would often see someone take out his pocket wallet, usually bulging with photographs, and muse over them, wishing he was back with his loved ones. Others might become interested in the photographs and soon everyone would gather round as the pictures were passed around for inspection. Every soldier I ever knew carried a pocket wallet like this, with pictures of home. And it did us no harm at all to indulge ourselves from time to time with nostalgic thoughts of our families and friends; in fact, it was essential to keep us within the bounds of sanity, and to remind us that the hellish world we had become accustomed to was *not* the real world at all, but only a gruesome nightmare that had to be endured before we could wake up to find ourselves once more in the bosom of our families.

Peace, to us at this time, seemed a very long way away, and our morale was not improved by constant shouts of '*hoch, hoch!*' (a 'hilarious' German greeting), many times repeated, coming from the German trenches, and Very lights (a type of flare) going up like fireworks all along their line. This was May 1918. We did not know at the time the cause of their jubilation; we only learned later that another of our allies, the Romanians, had collapsed.

The defeat of the Romanians was indeed bad news. We all knew what it meant: more enemy troops freed to divert and fight against us. I can remember trying to stay in a positive mind about it. 'Well, we stopped 'em last time, so why shouldn't we do it again?' Around the same time, we had also heard that American troops would soon be joining the war, so we continued to hope that they would arrive in time to assist us when the next offensive began. As it turned out, they were more urgently needed to help the French further south, but, of course, this indirectly helped us, because the troops released from Romania were not diverted to fight the British. So, things went on as before – for a little while, at any rate.

Around late June or early July 1918, there was a change. Our Division was situated in a 'bulge' of the fighting line, although we did not know it at the time. Men in the front line were often misled in this way, as the section of the line one was fighting on appeared straight enough from the ground, but could actually be much closer than other sections to the enemy line. Such was ours, and we had orders to withdraw in order to shorten the line, thus preventing the enemy from encircling us by attacking our flank and cutting us off. In a manoeuvre such as this the machine guns were responsible for any covering fire necessary for an orderly withdrawal.

The forward troops were to retire 'through' us, while our machine guns were placed in strategic positions along the whole of the front at distances varying from 100 yards to 200 yards and sometimes more, the intervening spaces being totally unprotected. This was always a tricky manoeuvre for a divisional commander, as liaison had to be complete between all guns, and each individual gun commander had to maintain contact with the gun on his left and the gun on his right. We had to communicate via a prearranged signal during daylight, as it was actually more hazardous to do so at night because of the likelihood of encountering a German patrol. It was the duty of the machine gun officer or his sergeant to visit each gun at intervals during the night. There were four guns between us, so we arranged to take two each. Each section of four machine guns was also allocated a platoon of riflemen to provide bayonet cover, if necessary.

It was here that I saw the strangest wound I ever knew a man to sustain. While I was on a visit to the gun on my right, one of the gunners was sitting in the trench, covered in blood. Fortunately, it looked much worse than it actually was. A German sniper had shot a hole in the front of the man's helmet, and by all the laws of nature, ballistics and physics, the bullet should have passed right through his head and killed him instantly. In actual fact the bullet had turned upwards and passed between his hair and the underside of his helmet. It had made a ridge some three-quarters of an inch high on his helmet, and then wounded him in the back of his neck and his shoulder. It was not a serious wound, but was sufficient to require his removal from the trenches. I had heard of cases where men had received a permanent 'parting' in their hair from a bullet, but never one so fantastic as a wound in the back of the neck from a bullet entering the *front* of the helmet.

In that part of France there were many small farms and cottages still more or less occupied by civilians, indicating the extent of the German offensive of the recent months. People had not moved out because there had been no heavy bombardments by the enemy in that area to date. It was not surprising, therefore, that there was a certain amount of small livestock, such as poultry, running around, although the heavier stock, such as horses, cattle and sheep had by then been evacuated by their owners once they had heard we would be withdrawing from the area.

We could see a few chickens picking and scratching for food, but we could not move from our positions in daylight to catch one without giving away our location to the enemy. It was very tempting though. Heartily sick and fed up with bully beef, we all knew that chicken for dinner would have been very nice indeed, so it was with great regret that we had to abandon the idea. More fortunate was the gun team whose post was 200 yards on our right, in the grounds of a small farm-house. A pig walked of its own accord into the yard at the back of the house, out of the sight of the enemy. Needless to say, it was quickly dispatched with a jack-knife, and then cleaned and prepared by the men using their jack-knives, jam tins and anything that would scrape off the hair. They must have killed the pig at about seven o'clock in the morning, but we knew nothing of it until about nine o'clock, when their Lance Corporal came over to us (by devious ways to avoid being seen by the enemy), and imagine our surprise when he dumped a huge joint of fresh pork onto our ammunition box!

'Where on earth's this come from?' I asked. (My language might have been slightly more colourful.)

He told us the whole story, and we had a good laugh about it, although there was more than one expression of sympathy for the poor pig.

'So, how are we going to cook it?' I asked next, a little warily, remembering my last culinary attempt with the mutton fat and jam pudding.

In our very early training we had received instruction in making a field oven. Up to then we had not had to make one, so we decided our training should be put to the test. We managed to build one, of sorts, in a low bank, sheltered from the enemy's view. The biggest problem, however, was to make a fire that would burn without giving off smoke, as smoke, of course, would alert the enemy to our position. We overcame this by breaking up ammunition boxes and then paring down the wood into thin slivers, almost like shavings, an operation which engaged the whole gun team, with the exception of the sentry, for several hours. We kept the fire continually blazing, with very little smoke, until we were satisfied the pork was cooked. It was all guesswork of course, but even if we had had the benefit of advice from the Savoy's master chef I am quite sure it would not have looked more appetising or smelled nicer to us, living as we did on our very monotonous diet of hard tack and bully. It was a truly lovely sight with its beautifully crisp crackling.

To go with the pork we had only the usual hard biscuits, but each of us had taken the precaution some hours before of putting three or four of them in a mess tin where they had swollen and gone soft enough, like porridge, for us to eat easily. It was a delicious meal – the best I had enjoyed, personally, since joining up. And we ate up every bit.

It was about an hour later that we all started to feel a bit poorly. We reckoned it was probably due to all the fat we had eaten, or perhaps the freshness of the meat; after all, the leg had still been running around attached to the pig only six hours before! Fortunately we all had strong stomachs and soon recovered without having to pay too many extra trips to the latrine (usually just a hole in the trench, and not a place to linger unnecessarily).

Our officer was not with the gun team that day. We waited for him to come to us after dark, when we would learn whether we were to stay in that position for another day or make a further move back. As it turned out, we were to stay in place another 24 hours.

This new officer, who had replaced Lieutenant Van Someren, was not long out from England. He was a very good officer, but quite inexperienced in actual warfare. When in doubt about tactics and such matters he would consult with the officer of the Notts and Derbys Platoon, who were accompanying our Section of machine guns. When it was something concerning our own men, or the task in hand, he always came to seek my opinion before acting, which I very much appreciated.

Up to this time, our withdrawal had been almost without incident. Certainly, the enemy did not seem over-anxious to come forward. The daily procedure was to send two men back to HQ each night in order to get instructions for the following 24 hours, the men being expected to return before daybreak. On this particular occasion, the men whose turn it was, Privates Spencer and Chatwin, had not returned by daybreak. We became anxious about their safety, but took the optimistic view that they had just been delayed and, not being able to reach our post before dawn, had decided to wait until nightfall. This was not the case, however, for during the afternoon, we saw two lone figures appear on the distant skyline. As they got nearer, we could recognise them with the aid of field glasses, and we thought how foolhardy they were to risk their lives by exposing themselves in the open. Our hopes for their safe arrival were shattered when they got to within 200–300 yards of us.

They had been spotted. One solitary shell came over and exploded with a terrible 'kerr-rrump' right between the two of them. When the cloud of black smoke cleared away, there was no sign of them. They had disappeared, and we all thought they must have been killed, as it seemed impossible for them to have survived a shell bursting at their very feet. Imagine our surprise, therefore, when one of the men, Spencer, crawled into our trench about an hour later. His injuries appeared to be mental rather than physical – he was trembling and totally incoherent – but miraculously he was not wounded. It was also a miracle for him to have retained the sagacity to find his way back to us. The state he was in, he might well have wandered off in any direction.

We laid him down and made him as comfortable as possible, and tried to reassure him that everything would be all right. When he became a little calmer, I asked him what happened to Chatwin. The question seemed to terrify him and he covered his face. Then he started repeating, 'He's blown to bits! He's blown to bits!'

The officer, as I have said before, was new to actual warfare, and this experience visibly affected him, as it would anyone who had not seen such things before, unlike the rest of us. He was talking to me about

Chatwin and his probable fate, when I suddenly became possessed with the conviction that he was lying out there somewhere, wounded and in need of help. My feeling was more than just conviction; it was a compulsive urge that I *must* go. I also experienced that same feeling of divine protection I had previously had in Bapaume in 1916; I *knew* I would not be harmed in going out to Chatwin.

I announced my intention to the officer. Naturally, he was reluctant to give his permission for me to go, as shelling was going on all around us now, but I was so convinced I would find Chatwin that eventually he let me go. An infantry officer who had heard our conversation told his stretcher-bearer to go with me to help carry Chatwin back.

On reaching the vicinity of the incident, I called out, 'Where are you, Chatwin?', and, to my delight, I received an answer back, 'Here I am, Sarge!' I was surprised to find we were quite near to him. His first words when he saw me were, 'I knew it was you who was coming, Sarge.' The significance of those words did not occur to me at the time; I was too concerned with finding out the extent of his wounds. He lay in a shell hole, with just his head and part of his shoulders protruding above the water that filled the hole. The water was stained red with his blood. I put my hands under his armpits to lift him out, and as his body came clear of the water he shrieked with pain, so much so that I was forced to let him slide back into the water. It was obvious that the icy cold of the water was helping to kill his pain. It was also obvious that he did not have long to live. His wounds were fearful: his one leg was missing, the other shattered from the knee downwards, and his left arm was broken.

I did not tell him the extent of his wounds. I just said to him, 'Chatwin, we'll soon have you out. Now you might be out of action for a while, so give me your home address and I'll write to your family and tell them you've been wounded.' I wrote it down and then asked him if there was anything in particular he would like me to say. His strange words are engraved on my mind and are verbatim. He said, 'Tell my mother I love her and tell my Dad that, with all his faults, I forgive him.'

My stretcher-bearer friend was standing near all the time I was talking to Chatwin. We talked of God, at least *I* did, and I talked in a manner which I would never have thought myself capable. I told him how Christ had died to save us all and that all who believed in Him would not die but have everlasting life. I was not sure where the words came from; my endeavour was to soothe him while I thought what to do. While he lay in the water he was not in pain, but he was deathly pale and every few minutes he would close his eyes and I would think he was dead. But no, he would open his eyes wide again and ask me something and I would continue talking to him. Such courage he showed as he waited to die I had never seen before or since.

On one of the short periods of consciousness, he looked me in the eye and said, 'Get me out of here, Sarge. I don't want to die in a shell hole.'

'Who says you're going to die?' I said. 'Alright, I'm going to get you out.' This dread of dying in a shell hole of water was shared by every soldier who had seen the corpses lying in water-filled shell holes. Countless injured men, who might otherwise have lived, drowned in the filthy water before they could be brought out.

I then turned to my colleague and asked him to talk to Chatwin while I went to find someone to fetch him out. In the ordinary way, I should only have had to go along a trench a little way to find a Red Cross unit, but in a situation like we found ourselves in I knew I would probably have to go back half a mile or more to get help. But luck was with me. After searching some empty trenches and dugouts about 100 yards back, I suddenly came across a small unit of Royal Army Medical Corps, consisting of a Sergeant and a few men. I told the Sergeant we had a badly wounded man up front and that I wanted them to come and help fetch him. He asked me about the extent of the man's wounds and I told him what I had seen, to which he answered, 'Oh, it's no use going to get him. He's going to die anyway.'

Such was the attitude of men hardened to suffering and death in this terrible war, I suppose, but this lack of basic humanity made me really angry, and I told him it was his *duty* to fetch the man. 'I'm not a medical man,' I said, 'but it's not for you or me to say whether or not he lives or dies. He needs help and you *must* come.'

The Sergeant was eventually persuaded, and he came with me him-self, as well as bringing two of his men with him. When we got back to Chatwin, he was still conscious, but he had sadly deteriorated since I had left him.

'You'll soon be all right now, old pal,' I said. He tried to smile, then went quiet.

The RAMC Sergeant looked at Chatwin and announced, 'He's gone.' Then, suddenly, Chatwin opened his eyes and shouted, 'Who's gone? I ain't gone! Hurry up and get me out of here!', then lapsed again into unconsciousness.

The Sergeant was still inclined to leave him in the hole, but I cut him short. I told him in no uncertain manner that I would not allow him and his men to leave without Chatwin. So, they managed to heave him out and put him on the stretcher. They took him away, still uncon-scious, and, as we learned later, he died two hours afterwards. Was it a waste of time? I didn't think so, because at least he didn't die in that shell hole.

Our colleagues at the machine-gun post had been watching us all the time. They told us that we had been an hour and twenty minutes with Chatwin, all that time exposed to the enemy. It had not seemed that long to me, being in the state of mind I was: I had been certain all the time that no danger existed for me or my colleague. I must have some way conveyed my mood to my Notts and Derby companion, for he never flinched all the way through the ordeal either.

Three questions arose for me from this episode: firstly, why, after Spencer's insistence that Chatwin had been blown to bits, did my mind become imbued with the certainty that he was still alive? Secondly, how did Chatwin know that it would be me who would go out to him? Thirdly, why did the Germans not fire a single shot at us during the whole period we were out there, while at the same time they were shelling heavily to our right and to our left and behind us?

Many theories could be advanced to explain my intuitions or pre-monitions on that day. A sixth sense, ESP, call it what you will, could be cited as the reason, but I don't believe that was it: I have made far too

many blunders in my lifetime to claim that I have ever possessed anything like a sixth sense. I truly believe that, as with the other instances
I have already described, there was a divine inspiration directing my
actions. I am certain that if it were possible to obtain the reminiscences
of all of the survivors of the First World War, many of them would tell
of similar experiences.

When our rearguard action finally ended and we joined the main
forces, we were allowed a short rest behind the lines, during which
time I wrote to Chatwin's mother telling her as gently as possible how
her son had died. Although I had witnessed so much death in my time
in the trenches and had, of necessity, become hardened to it – we all
had – Private Chatwin's death had affected me profoundly. At the same
time as I wrote to Chatwin's mother, I also wrote an unusually long
letter home on the same subject; that letter, as well as being unusually
long, was unusually poignant, and my family were deeply moved by it.
It also affected my brother-in-law, Percy Eagleton, who had recently
married my young sister, Nellie; so much so, that he had my pencil-
written letter typed out and he gave it to my sister Ada. Ada still had the
letter some five or six years ago (around 1960), when I was able to read
it again. Had I realised at that time that I would be writing these memoirs, I would certainly have borrowed it to repeat here; now, sadly, she
no longer has it. Incidentally, I never received an answer to my letter to
Private Chatwin's mother. I therefore came to the conclusion that his
father and mother did not get along very well. The boy's reference to
his father's faults may not have been well received, but I felt it was my
duty to quote his 'last words' verbatim.

   During the brief rest we had at the end of our eventful rearguard
action, the exploit concerning Privates Spencer and Chatwin got
around the Company. The story lost nothing in its telling; in fact, it
gained so much in its repetition that some went so far as to suggest that
I should have been awarded the Victoria Cross! I hesitate to mention
this fact as it may seem that I was exceptionally brave, or am endeav-
ouring to make it appear so. I only mention it because it was actually

said to me, personally, by an experienced officer, who said that had he been there he would have made a very favourable report on it. I can remember suggesting to this officer that, while thanking him for his great compliment, the story had been blown out of proportion.

I would be less than human if I had not felt enormously flattered by all the compliments showered on me. But, at the same time, I must keep to the truth and assert that if I did a brave deed then it was not of my own volition, but under the influence and inspiration of divine protection – I really believed that, although I am not a particularly religious man. If anyone deserved an award in that instance it was my companion, the stretcher-bearer, who was out there with me all the time, and was not aware of the divine protection! I just *knew* I was not in danger, but my comrade did not, which, to my mind, makes all the difference.

CHAPTER ELEVEN

WOUNDED AT MOUNT KEMMEL, YPRES, THE MILITARY MEDAL – THE ARMISTICE

The rearguard action I have described was not, as it seemed, carried out because of enemy pressure, but as a tactical manoeuvre in order to straighten the line in preparation for a general assault on the enemy positions. On 8 August 1918, offensive operations of varying degrees commenced all along the Allied lines, which were to continue, as it transpired, until the end of the war. By early August, we had moved from the Somme and were back on the Ypres Salient. Our unit took up positions near Mount Kemmel.

Two Americans were with our Section, placed with us to gain experience from 'seasoned' troops. One of our American guests was a Sergeant from Brooklyn. He was a pleasant chap and we had some very interesting conversations while waiting for our turn to 'go in'. Our last conversation ended with an invitation from him for me to go to New York, and he promised me a whale of a time – after the war, of course. I did not see him again, however, as our Section was allocated the task of preparing two machine-gun positions in no-man's-land. This task took us two or three nights to complete. We advised the Sergeant not to come with us on the mission, as we thought the risk was too great for him, inexperienced as he was. We thought there was no need to risk his life unnecessarily, though he was willing enough himself.

The gun positions we were preparing lay about midway between our own front line and the German front line, so we were not more than 50–70 yards from the enemy, and our work had to be done as silently as possible. When the Very lights went up we had to freeze for the duration of their light, which was about fifteen seconds. (A Very light was fired from a special pistol and provided a very bright light hanging in the air, lighting up the surroundings for a short period.)

These gun positions had to be ready for the night of 9 August as our troops were to make a raid on the enemy positions in order to gain information about the enemy's strength and intentions. Our job was to provide enfilade fire (a volley of gunfire directed along the line from end to end) in order to keep the Germans in their trenches, or to trap them if they crawled into their own barbed wire defences to await the raiding party. This was a trick often used by both sides. So, one of our guns was laid on the wire and the other on the enemy trenches, thus making them keep their collective head down, the artillery barrage doing the rest.

The raid was scheduled to take place at midnight on the 9th, all watches being synchronised a short time beforehand, precision being the essence of the exercise. There was to be a nine-minute bombardment of the enemy positions, beginning at 11.51pm and ending at midnight precisely. Our orders were that as soon as the artillery opened up, our two machine guns were to open up, and then cease fire after precisely nine minutes, to allow the raiding party to go over the top to assault the enemy trenches. As I have already said, precision timing was crucial, as once the raiding party had gone over the top they would be in our direct line of fire, so it was absolutely vital that we had ceased firing before the raiding party moved.

Everything was quiet just before the raid. The enemy was suspicious though, which was shown by the number of Very lights they were using. The officer who was in charge of our two guns (yet another 'new face' whose name I unfortunately cannot recall), although he had been in action before and I thought would be cool under pressure, seemed anxious and kept looking at his watch and comparing his time with mine. He was very tense and on edge, as I suppose we all were. The minutes were ticking by. Five minutes to go! Three minutes to go! One minute to go! That last minute always seemed longer than the others. Then the hellish cacophony began with a blaze of artillery fire, to which we added our own deadly chatter of machine-gun fire. The noise was terrific – bedlam – like a thousand thunderstorms rolled into one. I can recall clearly the faces of the men around me on that night, flushed and excited, as we fired our guns at the Jerries.

The bombardment continued; it seemed to last forever. Then, suddenly, our officer went berserk. He climbed up onto the parapet yelling wild, unnecessary orders at us, and waving his arms about. Our two guns were firing to the very limit, and belt after belt of rounds went through the guns, each belt containing 250 rounds of ammunition; and, considering that each gun could fire at the rate of 600 rounds a minute, allowing for reloading, we must have fired something like 9,000–10,000 bullets into those Germans.

Time was getting on; taking a glance at my watch I could see there was only one minute to go before cease fire. I held up one finger and yelled to the officer, 'One minute to go, Sir!', but he didn't seem to understand me. He was shouting, hysterical, obviously out of control. He kept yelling 'Keep firing! Keep firing!', and was waving his arms about like a madman.

Then the artillery bombardment stopped as suddenly as it had started. This meant that our men would now be getting out of their trenches and in a few seconds would be in our line of fire. 'Keep firing! Keep firing!' shouted our officer in his madness, but I knew if we did so, we would soon be killing our own men. I was in a terrible quandary; I could not openly disobey an officer's orders, even if he was quite clearly insane. I had to think fast. I was standing next to one of the guns, and I gave the adjusting wheel a little turn, which raised the muzzle of the gun, so that it would fire into the air and over the heads of our men. I indicated to one of my colleagues to do the same with the other gun; he, of course, could see my motive and lost no time in doing so.

We continued to fire. It seemed as if we had been firing for hours over our allotted time, but was only about two minutes in actual fact, when the officer suddenly came to his senses, realised the bombardment had stopped and finally ordered us to cease fire. It had only been two minutes, but nevertheless, I knew that extra firing could have caused much havoc among our raiding party and could possibly have ruined the entire exercise. We waited to hear when the raid was over, and we sincerely hoped that it had been successful.

We could relax a little now. I decided to take a quick look into the darkness to see if I could see anything or anyone moving. Peering over the parapet I suddenly felt a terrific blow on my face, just as if I had been struck by an iron bar. I couldn't think what it was for a second, then I realised I had been hit. It is said that as a person is drowning his whole life passes before him, well, it wasn't my whole life which passed before me; only two thoughts as I was losing consciousness: Am I dead? No, I ain't! I tried to fix my eyes on a tuft of grass, saying to myself over and over, 'That's grass, that's grass, that's grass,' – how many times, I don't know. Things went black; a great shutter, as black as the Styx, started to come down in front of me, lower and lower as I kept repeating to myself, 'That's grass!'

The chink of light below the great shutter became less and less until it was the thinness of a hair, but still I could see part of that tuft of grass. Then, wonderfully, it began to lift, very slowly, with each moment the strip of light increasing again, until I was fully conscious. I was still standing up, looking at that wonderful tuft of grass! I don't think that I completely lost consciousness, but must have been very close to it, and had I not fixed my mind on that tuft of grass I believe I should have fallen. As it was, I was leaning forward against the parapet of the trench.

The next thing I realised was that I was covered in blood, from my head right down to my boots – and there was a lot of it. I felt tentatively around for my wound, and at the same time the officer came up to me to say something and a Very light went up, bathing us in its glow. The moment he saw my face covered in blood, he stopped in the middle of his sentence and said, 'Good God, Sergeant! You've been hit!'

He was quite back to normal following his previous moment of madness, and was very concerned about my wound. I remember feeling a sense of exhilaration that I was still alive; the feeling of having looked death in the eye, so to speak, and survived is something that must be experienced to be fully appreciated.

It was a near thing. The bullet had hit me high up on the cheekbone and along the temple and my right eye. The wound itself was a gash of about two inches long from the point of my cheekbone and along the temple. Just a fraction of an inch closer to my eye and I would have been dead. It is a strange thing: I had always feared a bullet wound to the temple most of all, as being the one most likely to see me off, but this was not a serious wound; the bullet had grazed me rather than entered my skull. But, it must have seemed to the officer that my face was half blown away, considering the amount of blood there was. He insisted I go to the dressing station, the whereabouts of which we always noted before an action such as we had just completed. An ambulance was supposed to go to the dressing station at about 12.30 that night to pick up the wounded.

I did not want to go. I wanted to wait until dawn when we would all be leaving the post together, and anyway, I was feeling all right, but he insisted, saying that my wound needed attending to. So, off I went. When I arrived at the dressing station, they told me the ambulance had already left, so the men there put a dressing on my face. They didn't seem all that bothered about me and told me to make my own way back to HQ.

The prospect of walking all the way back to Company HQ was not a rosy one. It was seven miles back through trenches and over rough country, at least for the first two miles. However, it was not uncommon for us to march twenty miles or more in a day, so I thought that I should be able to manage seven. I was forgetting one thing, though: I had lost a great deal of blood, far in excess of what one would expect in a facial wound, and after the first few miles it began to tell on me. I was obliged to take frequent rests, and each time I came upon a sentry I stopped and took a rest and had a chat. Each sentry asked for news of the raid, but I only knew our part of it.

Later on my long walk, having gone through the trench system, I came to open country, such as it was with its gaunt trees and innumerable shell craters and, as I moved on I came to a wood which some time previously had received a heavy pounding, but nevertheless provided shelter from view for an American battalion which was camped there. This wood was about a mile and a half from my journey's end, and it was broad daylight by now. The camp had not yet risen so I only encountered their sentries, for whom, it seemed, I provided their first sight of battle-blood, for I was covered in it. They were sympathetic and wanted to help me, but I told them I did not have far to go and I wanted to go on, so I thanked them and carried on. I know I could have stopped there for a while, but really I did not feel up to answering all the inevitable questions.

Pushing on, I eventually arrived at HQ at about seven in the morning. It had taken me nearly six hours to cover just seven miles. I was all in. Of course, what they should have done back at the dressing station was to have held me there until I was fit enough to walk that distance, but they could not have cared less about me.

At Company HQ all was quiet except for one sentry and the Company cooks who had just brewed their first tea, some of which they offered to me – it tasted like the elixir of life! Never was a drink of tea more welcome, or tasted so good. Then the cooks made me breakfast, which put new life into me, and all I wanted then was to lie down and sleep for about a week. Unfortunately, I could not go and lie down until I had reported to the Medical Officer and to the Company Commander, Captain Cowley.

The MO examined me and said, 'That was a close shave, Sergeant, but the wound isn't serious.' Then I went to report to the CC. He told me he knew all about it by field telephone, but assumed I had gone to hospital in the ambulance – which I should have done, had I been five minutes earlier at the dressing station. He also told me that the raid had been a great success and that our two machine guns had done a splendid job in preventing German reinforcements coming up, and this had been verified by German prisoners captured in the raid. This meant that the extra elevation I and my comrade had put on the guns, after the official cease fire, had accidentally, but fortuitously stopped the Germans coming up to drive back our raiding parties.

The next day, after having a good sleep and getting a clean rig-out, I felt great but I had a lovely black eye, which I thought strange after losing so much blood. My cheekbone was very tender; the bullet had obviously grazed the bone, which was rather painful, but a small matter, all things considered. I was told I should stay at HQ for a few days to rest – I wasn't going to argue! Later I was informed that I was to go away to a convalescent camp for two weeks – better and better!

The convalescent camp was at a small village a few miles north of Boulogne, called Wimereux. It was a charming little place only a few hundred yards from a beautiful sandy beach, from which we could make out the white cliffs of Dover – a sight for very sore eyes after months surrounded by nothing but death and destruction. The officer in charge of the camp was the kind of officer every soldier dreams about serving under. He was elderly, by our standards, probably nearing 50 and was everybody's 'uncle'. He paraded us the morning after my arrival and addressed us something like this:

> I know what you boys have been through and why you've been sent here, so your stay will be as pleasant as you, yourselves make it. All that I require of you is that you behave in a soldierly manner and cause no trouble to anyone inside or outside the camp.
>
> There will be one parade only each day, which will be Roll Call. After that you have the day to do as you wish. You will be on your honour. If anyone gets into trouble he will be sent back to his unit immediately. So far, no-one has been sent back. It is now up to you.

He was a great fellow and he saw to it that we were all well fed and looked after by the medical staff. I soon realised how lucky I was to have been sent to that particular camp. I heard that some convalescent camps were so strictly run that the wounded couldn't wait to get back to the fighting.

I remember those as idyllic days. There was no 'rank': everyone was addressed by their first names. Some who were a bit wobbly on their pins were helped by others of us who were more able to go and enjoy the lovely golden sands and the wonderful 'starkers' sea bathing, which we happily indulged in without a stitch on. It seemed like the perfect place to swim, free from prying eyes; that is, until one day we saw strolling along the beach from the direction of Boulogne, two girls carrying baskets of tomatoes. It was panic stations! We made a concerted rush up the beach to our clothes, which were at least 100 yards away but suddenly seemed much further. We ran faster from those girls than we would ever have done from the Germans.

It seemed that the girls went into the village nearly every day to sell their tomatoes and were not a bit embarrassed at encountering naked men. It was us (big, brave, fighting men) who got red-faced and flustered. We saw them on many days after that but rather than keep running for our clothes we decided to stay 'under cover' in the water instead.

It was during my stay at the convalescent camp that I learned I had been awarded the Military Medal. The news reached me via a re-addressed letter from home which had my name on the envelope and the letters MM. When I returned to my unit, I was sent for by Captain Cowley, who congratulated me on the award. He admitted that he was disappointed it was only the Military Medal, as he had tried to get me a higher award, the Distinguished Conduct Medal. The DCM would have carried with it a small bounty of twenty pounds and a pension. He told me that he had received several favourable reports on my conduct over the past few months, and specifically mentioned the Chatwin affair and the last engagement in which I was wounded. He told me that the officer who had been in charge of the two guns at Kemmel had told Captain Cowley how he had lost control and that my 'presence of mind' had saved the situation and potentially many lives.

When I received the medal and citation, which was not until after the war was over, the citation read 'For gallantry and devotion to duty when, although wounded, you remained in command of a machine gun', and signed by General Marden.

I would like to say here that I thought my officer's behaviour was very gentlemanly in admitting his failure in the Kemmel engagement. It would have been easy for him to have claimed all the credit for the much-praised part our two guns played in the successful raid; after all, the kind of temporary loss of control he displayed was not uncommon in such terrifying bombardments.

And my medal? Well, it might be useful to say a little about how awards of decorations were made. There seemed to be two different ways. The first, in a case where a particular unit such as a battalion, company or platoon have distinguished themselves in a certain battle or engagement with the enemy, the General Staff, or the divisional commander would award a certain number of decorations such as the Distinguished Service Order and Military Cross to officers, and the Distinguished Conduct Medal and Military Medal to NCOs and men. These would be distributed by the unit's commanding officer after consultation with his junior officers, to determine who should be the recipients. The Victoria Cross did not come under this heading. It was always an individual award, available to all ranks for the highest acts of bravery. Secondly, an award could be made through recommendation in a special report made to the commanding officer by someone on the spot, be it the officer, NCO or private, about another individual who they consider has done something exceeding his line of duty. The CO would then send on a report to GHQ, who would then decide if an award would be made.

I think you will agree with me that my award came under the second heading – but there is an inside story to all this. At the time of the Chatwin incident – or rather after it – it appears that the CO did not receive any report of it from the officer in charge, who, it will be remembered, was inexperienced, and that the CO only learned about it through rumour. Apparently, he was a little put out at not knowing soon enough to be able to send on a report of the incident himself. I was given this piece of information by the orderly room clerk, a corporal, whose job it was to pass on all the orders and instructions concerning the Company – he was, of course, bound to secrecy!

When I came back from the convalescent camp, wearing my MM ribbon on my uniform, the clerk called me over and congratulated me, and then told me the story of how it came about, whilst, of course, swearing me to secrecy. In effect, he explained that because the CO had not learned of my conduct in the Chatwin incident soon enough to report to GHQ, he had given orders that I was to be 'watched' and was to be reported on in everything I did in order to find something on which he *could* make a favourable report to GHQ. Then the Kemmel incident came up. I had had to take command because the officer had lost control, but in the citation for my award it said 'that, although wounded, you remained in command of a machine gun'. Of course, this was incorrect: it indicates that I was wounded *before* the action was over, rather than *after*. However, it provided my CO with sufficient material to get the Military Medal for me (although, sadly, not quite enough for a DCM). So, really, I got the medal for what I tried to do for poor Chatwin.

And that is the story of my Military Medal. My only real disappointment about the whole thing was that I never actually had it pinned on me by my CO – it was sent to me in the post after the war.

When I returned from my two-week convalescence around the end of August, the Company had been relieved by the Americans, probably the ones whose camp I had passed through previously, and so my comrades were preparing to move to another front further to the south-east, on the Somme. We did a terrific amount of marching during the next few weeks, and plenty of fighting; in fact, we were either marching or fighting continuously until the end of October. The entire Division was completely worn out with fatigue. The casualties had been enormous, so much so, that our Company had lost every one of its senior officers, among them Captain Cowley. There were no officers higher in rank than a 2nd Lieutenant. The whole Division was withdrawn for a rest, during which time we received some reinforcements – not nearly enough – among whom was a full lieutenant, just out from England who had never fired a shot except in training. This man (I forget his name, which is probably just as well), because of his rank, became the company commander, the senior officer of our Company, and incomparable to Captain Cowley and other good officers who had commanded us and died fighting alongside us.

I want to say at this point that 'living' as I am inside my mind as I write these memoirs in order to bring up the memories, I find I cannot recall any other specific incidents (although there must have been many) that occurred between the end of August and the end of October. During that period of the war, some of the heaviest fighting took place, and according to books about the First World War, the front, from the coast to the Swiss border, was in a state of turmoil. I certainly remember Kemmel, for obvious reasons, and I remember Bohain that November, and the Armistice; however, there are over 100 kilometres between the two places, so we must have fought on several fronts during that time. I know that we fought in three major battles (Epéhy, St Quentin Canal, and the Selle), but not a single incident can I now recall which I could categorically state took place during that period. And yet, if someone were to remind me of an incident that I had been associated with, it would come back to me quite clearly. I know this because an instance of this occurred in 1927 – nine years later – when I bumped into a cousin of mine from Bloxwich, Ernie Smith.

As we stood chatting in Bloxwich that day, Ernie mentioned something that indicated he had been in the Army. I said immediately, 'I didn't know you had joined up too, Ernie.' He looked hard at me for a moment and said, 'What do you mean, you didn't know I joined up? We only went and met each other in France! Surely you ain't forgot?' To say I was embarrassed at his remarks was putting it mildly, for I had not the least idea what he was talking about. I told him I was sorry but could not remember meeting him. I asked him to tell me about the incident in the hope it might come back to me.

He explained that he had been home on leave and, on returning to France, had arrived with two others at a camp which was occupied by our Company. Describing his arrival he said, 'When we arrived at your camp, we stood outside your orderly room while someone went to find that day's Orderly Sergeant. When he came it was you! When you saw who I was, you nearly shook my hand off!'

Slowly, the scene began to take shape in my mind. Ernie and his two companions had needed a billet for the night. I had sent the other two to a tent with some other chaps, but insisted Ernie share my tent. 'You're staying with me, Ernie lad,' I had said to him. It was a very strange feeling to see the picture of the incident unfold itself as Ernie was telling me, like rolling up the blind of a darkened window. To meet someone you knew in France was really something, but to meet a relative should have been unforgettable. I have wondered since many times what other incidents of that period are locked away in my subconscious.

In self-analysis it seems to me that I could have been suffering from delayed amnesia, caused by the bullet which struck me in the temple. Another theory, put forward now by my daughter, Edith, on whose views I place great credence, might have been that the relentless fighting had finally proved too much for my sub-conscious mind, which simply refused to record or recall any more of the horrors I had witnessed. Whether either of these theories is correct or not, the fact remains that it happened, and it might also, in some measure, account for the fact that the names of many of my associates do not come easily to me. I was actually boasting about my memory a chapter or so back, and I think with good reason, except for the 'blank' period described above.

It was the end of October and we were still on our month's 'rest'. Fierce battles were still raging all along the front, but we thought that at least we had done our part for another couple of weeks. Little did we suspect how close the end was. In the first week of November 1918 our rest was interrupted when we were ordered up the line in support of a major offensive at Landrecies, near Morval Wood on the Somme. We were to go forward with the first attacking troops and to consolidate at the first objectives. If our attacking troops broke through the German defences (which they did) we were to remain in our positions until nightfall, then withdraw. This we did, then continued with our rest at our camp in Bohain.

Our new CO thought we needed gingering up a bit while we were on our 'rest', and treated us to a programme of parades as though we were raw recruits. He even instituted 'evening lectures' (by himself, of course) which, needless to say, were as boring as he was.

Then came the morning of 11 November, Armistice Day. We were busily marching up and down a piece of waste ground, when suddenly we could hear the sounds of jubilation coming from the direction of Bohain. Word, of course, had been going around since the previous day of a possible Armistice, so when we heard the sounds, we fervently hoped it was true. I remember clearly that we couldn't quite take it in, but the noise and then the sound of a band coming towards us from the town, certainly raised a few hopes.

So, did our new CO let us go and see what was happening? Not Pygmalion likely! He seemed as unperturbed as though the people of Bohain were celebrating a Sunday School treat rather than the end of the most devastating and bloody war of all time. Our dinner break came at last and we went to join the troops of the 6th Division who were already celebrating. So, then we knew – it was over!

I found that it was all too much to take in at once, after so many years and so much bloodshed. The war was over! I remember trying to imagine what it was going to be like not having to go back to the trenches ever again, not having to witness any more death, stand in mud up to my waist and listen to the cries of the dying. I couldn't quite take in that I would never again have to breathe in the stench of those trenches, or have my ears assaulted by the cacophony of shelling, or feel that terrible dread that I might be dead at any moment. My mind raced with it all. 'No more hard tack and bully!' I remember someone shouting, although probably not that politely. I agreed with him; personally, I never wanted to see another tin. (In fact, I never could face bully beef again after the war; I still can't.)

We walked on towards Bohain, still wondering if it really was true. But then we could see the band marching up and down the main street. Flags and bunting had suddenly appeared, as if by magic. Women and children were laughing and crying all at the same time, and soon the streets were full of soldiers and civilians; the main street was so full the band had to stop marching, so it stayed in one position and carried on playing there, for hours. It was a sight for very sore eyes!

It did not occur to any of us that we would be required to parade that afternoon, or that any officer, realising that the war was over, would want it. But, our new CO did! So, we had to go on parade in the afternoon, while everyone else was in the town enjoying themselves, and he made us parade until dusk. I believe we were the only company in the entire Division (and probably the whole ruddy British Army) who were on parade that afternoon. Dusk came about four o'clock, and we were very relieved to see it. As there was about an hour or so to go before tea, we sergeants gathered in the mess, and all talk was of the Armistice. Even the antics of our new CO could not suppress our excitement at the news that the war was over.

After tea, we started cleaning ourselves up a bit in preparation for a night on the town, when a messenger came with a note from the CO addressed to the Orderly Sergeant, who I think was called Sergeant Macauley, a Scot with a fine sense of humour. His humour, however, was not apparent as he read out the note. It didn't make us laugh much either. It read something like this:

To all ranks; the men of 'C' Company will assemble in the lecture hall at 6p.m. to be addressed by the officers of the Company. Then, all Sergeants and full Corporals will assemble at – [this was a private house which had been used during the war as an office] to be lectured by myself.
Signed [whatever the wretched man's name was]
Commanding Officer, 'C' Company

Well, we were absolutely flabbergasted! We could not think what kind of lecture he thought would be of the faintest interest to us at that time – we wanted to go out and celebrate. We were quite sure he would have nothing pleasant to say; he was not that kind of man. We were soon to find out, when later that evening the sergeants and corporals had assembled in a bedroom about fifteen feet square with a blackboard in one corner. There were no chairs or any other furniture – just a blackboard.

The CO began his lecture by saying, 'Now that the Armistice is signed, I have no doubt that you men think the war is over, but it is not, and it is in all our interests to consider what we are going to do in 1919. I therefore propose to give you a lecture on "Our Strategy and Tactics for 1919".'

We all looked at one another in disbelief, and as the CO turned his back to draw some lines on the blackboard, a loud 'raspberry' issued from somewhere among us. He turned round sharply and exclaimed, 'Who was that?' There was dead silence, of course. Then another 'raspberry' sounded from a different part of the room, and when he looked in that direction, yet another one came from somewhere else. As he looked from one face to another to find the offender, he was met by blank stares – we were all as innocent as new-born babies.

He tried valiantly to continue with his lecture, but the conditions which we created for him, which could not have been more effective if we had rehearsed them (which we had not), made it impossible for him to carry on. At least he had the sense to give up and dismiss us.

Any other officer I have ever come across would have been livid to have been rebuffed in such a way; but then, no other officer would have forced us to stay in and listen to a boring lecture on Armistice night. He didn't seem to be angry so much as puzzled as to why we ignorant, low class people could be so ungracious as to reject his fascinating insights into strategy and tactics for 1919. He must have led a very sheltered life.

Personally, although I joined in with the rest and played my part in wrecking his lecture, I did feel a slight twinge of pity for him, because he did look a bit crestfallen. He must have recounted his experience with the other officers in the officers' mess, because I think they had a word with him; certainly, he was a bit less obnoxious after that.

It did occur to me at the time to wonder how this officer would have behaved under fire – anybody's guess, I suppose. He might even have turned out to be a brave man. A man's potential in war can never be gauged from ordinary life: under great stress, as in war, suddenly the weediest looking among us can possess the heart of a lion. Conversely, and I have seen this for myself, the big man with the jutting jaw can be the biggest coward.

CHAPTER TWELVE

MARCH TO THE RHINE – DEMOBILISATION

A few days after the Armistice, we set off on the Great March to the Rhine. The march took us from Bohain to Cologne, which according to my reckoning was roughly 300 kilometres. The first two or three days of marching was over devastated countryside and flattened villages and towns. It was a bleak landscape indeed. During one of our periodic 'halts' in this region, we saw something, battle-hardened as we were to the sight of dead bodies and graves, that saddened us all deeply. Just off to the side of the road where we were resting stood a wooden cross, made from two pieces of white boxwood nailed together bearing the inscription, written in indelible pencil,

Pte –

Killed in Action at 11.10 a.m.

on November 11th 1918

R.I.P.

None of us knew him, or how long he had been out there fighting for his king and country. He might have missed death by inches many times; we did not know. And we had seen so many deaths, so many graves, and this was just another; it might have been unremarkable in a land littered with makeshift memorials to the many who fell. But, we couldn't help but be touched by the irony of this death; this poor soul being killed ten minutes after hostilities had officially ceased.

Although this was the only instance I actually knew of where some-one had been killed after the Armistice, there must have been others too, as I well remember men boasting about having fired a 'few more shots for luck' when they heard of the Armistice. The Germans prob-ably did the same.

Continuing on our march, we gradually emerged into open coun-try, with proper roads and railways, green fields and trees. The trees were almost leafless as it was late autumn, but still beautiful in that they were whole and not splintered and broken like so many thousands of others which had become such a familiar sight to us. By the time we reached Namur in Belgium, we were becoming accustomed to the beauty of the countryside, but were not quite prepared for the magnificence of the banks of the river Meuse, as we crossed a bridge leading into Namur itself. The many, varying colours of autumn blended together to present a spectacular picture. I can remember remarking to someone at the time that it was the most magnificent view I had ever seen in my life.

Entering the town, we were greeted like conquering heroes, and there was hardly an individual who was not carrying some kind of home-made Union Jack. There were a few genuine ones too, which obviously had been kept well hidden from the Germans during their occupation. Even the children had made Union Jacks with coloured crayons and put them on little sticks to wave at us.

We rested for the night in Namur and took the opportunity to have a look around. There were no young men to be seen; they had been sent long ago to work in Germany, but the old men were pleased to show us around. Language was the great difficulty, which we tried to over-come with mime and gestures and shouting – just as the English still do today! The old man who escorted our little party took us, amongst other places, to a kind of courtyard where many executions had taken place. All 'spies' and people who refused to work for the Germans had been taken there to be shot. The disfigured walls with their splintered brickwork, caused by the bullets, provided mute evidence of the grisly use to which the courtyard had been put.

The scenes of jubilation and demonstrations of pleasure we had received in Namur were repeated in every town and village we passed through in Flanders and Belgium. Our schedule for this long march was that we marched for four days in succession, with distances varying according to the accommodation at the other end, then took one, sometimes two days rest. These rests, especially for the first 50 miles or so, were a Godsend, as our feet had become rather tender after the many months of daily application of whale oil in order to prevent the dreaded 'trench foot', a disease which sometimes resulted in amputation. The evil smelling whale oil had been a great boon in protecting our feet from the unpleasant effects of wading through trench mud for months on end, but had left our feet a bit 'delicate'.

As our feet became accustomed to the marching, however, there were fewer and fewer men 'falling out' because of sore feet. Those who did fall out would be picked up by the transport officer and allowed to ride on the gun limbers. It was always an unwritten point of honour in the Army that no man fell out unless he absolutely had to; any man who fell out without good reason was looked upon as a malingerer. So, sore feet prevailed!

In my Army life, I only ever came across one man who was a malingerer, and the least said about him the better, in my opinion. On the other hand, we had a man in our unit on that march who was so obviously ill that I advised him to drop out from the march and ride on the limbers. We were about two days march from the German frontier at the time. But, he would not give up, and he carried on until we reached the town of Malmédy, which was then the first town inside Germany (it is now part of Belgium). On realising he had crossed the frontier and set foot in Germany itself, he collapsed and had to be taken to hospital. He had realised his ambition, misguided though it may have been, but for sheer courage it was outstanding.

So, the Great March went on, with the regimental band at the head, and the sound of those inspiring marches they played was a tonic to us all. Mile after mile after mile we trudged with our 90-pound packs on our backs, getting wearier as each day wore on. Then suddenly the band would strike up, and it would seem that as the first drum rolls and the first notes rang out, some invisible hands had placed themselves under our packs, relieving us of the weight. It would bring out some last reserves of strength we were unaware we had, and enable us not only to march on but to actually enjoy it too – which I suppose was yet another victory of mind over matter.

As we marched into German towns, we were not received with the same enthusiasm as we were in Flanders and Belgium, nor did we expect it, but we were rather surprised to be greeted with courtesy and goodwill, as we had anticipated a certain amount of hostility. They were enemies no longer and they seemed to accept their position philosophically. In fact, it was generally agreed amongst ourselves that the German civilians were actually kinder to us than the French had ever been.

In only one case did we notice anything bordering on hostility. It was in a large pub on one of our rest days. We were enjoying ourselves with German civilians and generally 'whooping it up' when, from an upstairs room (presumably a club room) descended several bearded gentlemen wearing strange headgear, which I supposed was from some club or society. Thinking about it now, it looked not unlike the Klu Klux Klan's sinister get-up. We asked them to join us for a drink. They ignored us majestically and walked out into the night. We felt a little abashed at the snub, but we forgot it soon enough and returned to our partying.

I said 'we forgot it', but personally, I have never forgotten it, and I have wondered many times since if that was a sign of the spirit that festered in the German soul, which culminated in support for Adolf Hitler's regime, and which led, only twenty years later to the next bloodbath, the Second World War.

In another pub in another German town, we had a quite different experience. The landlord was a big fellow, an ex-soldier and only recently demobilised. There were four of us and no other customers in the place, and as we approached the bar he put down five glasses. Then he reached for a bottle containing a yellow liquid and invited us to join him in a glass of wine. He spoke fairly good English and emphasised that the drinks were on the house. Naturally, we were suspicious and made him take the first drink, for which we were a little shamefaced afterwards, when we realised he was only being friendly and wasn't trying to poison us. He took up his drink and drank it in one gulp, then treated us to a broad grin as he filled our glasses up. He did not seem a bit put out by our wary behaviour; in fact, he insisted on treating us to free drinks all evening. I think he was as pleased as we were that the war was over.

There was an organ in the room. Now, although I was not a profes-sional player – self-taught on the organ at home, if you remember – I could play sufficiently well by ear to knock off a few tunes without frightening the horses. I had not played since my last leave the previous March, and I was eager to try my hand at the German organ. I asked our host if I might play it and he said he would be delighted, so I began with 'Colonel Bogey', one of the marches I had memorised on our way there. The boys loved it, and, I must admit, I was rather surprised myself I could play it at my first attempt – that German wine was good stuff! All in all, I had memorised about fourteen marches along our march to the Rhine, so I gave them a bit of a show. Later, I played the waltz 'Over the Waves', which my host informed me was a German tune, and it mightily pleased him.

We were all highly in his favour by then and we got to talking about the war. He said he had been wounded. I asked him where and he replied, 'At Mount Kemmel last August, by several machine gun bullets.' Of course, my curiosity was aroused, so I asked him if he remembered the date. He said it had been early in August during a heavy raid the British made on German lines. Astounded, I told him that I had been wounded in the same raid! We were great pals by that time – we both might have been in the same army, judging from the friendship which had developed between us. This to my mind, just goes to prove that the bitterness and hatred in war is caused by propaganda and is often not shared by the men who actually do the fighting: another example of the absolute futility of war.

We were on the move again the next day, our flagging steps spurred along by the music from the band. We marched on for the next four days, when again we would take two days rest. Our next rest came at a pretty little village, where a colleague and I had a rather embarrassing experience. My pal and I had been billeted at a house, and that day it was washing day, with steam and the smell of soap suds heavy in the air. It reminded us that there might be chance of a bath if the woman of the house could be persuaded to save some hot water after she had finished her washing. To this end, we sought out a private who had been appointed interpreter to the Company.

Having found him, we took him back to our billet so that he could ask the lady if we could have a bath after she had finished her washing. Well, he couldn't have been the best interpreter in the world, for as we stood like a couple of dopes, listening but not knowing what was being said, but watching their faces as they talked, the woman seemed confused and more than a little embarrassed. We could not imagine why. In the end, our 'interpreter' told us that the woman had 'misunderstood his translation' and thought we were asking for *her* to bath us. Perish the thought!

Of course, misunderstandings like that one were bound to arise when you don't speak each other's language. We did, however, get our bath that evening, in a gigantic wooden tub. After we had finished clearing up, we invited the woman and her family into our room as a gesture of thanks and a desire to be friendly. And she didn't run a mile; she accepted very graciously and introduced all her family to us, the family consisting of herself, an old lady and two children, a boy and a girl, who were about twelve and fourteen. There was no man in the house, as could be expected. We all got along famously, especially with the children, who took a great interest in our language and military insignia, such as our cap badges, shoulder numerals, stripes and such like. We exchanged inspections of each others' photographs, trying to explain in each others' language who the people were. It was a very enjoyable evening, not that any of us understood much of what was said, but the spirit of friendliness was there.

After one more day in that village, we were on the march again. The next day's march was a long one of over twenty miles. On long marches such as that, it was an unwritten law of etiquette that the commanding officer, who rides his horse at the head of the column, gets down from his horse when he realises that his troops are getting weary. But not our new CO. He would always ride out a march from beginning to end. Marching behind him mile after mile, day after day, we were used to seeing his back, his thin neck and his protruding ears. On that day, as we became progressively leg-weary, the sight of his ears proved too much for one of the boys, who suddenly yelled out, 'Some people have ears for music; others just have them to keep their cap on.'

The CO turned around in his saddle, not saying a word, and gazed into a sea of blank faces. He turned back, rode a little further, then stopped, dismounted, and walked along with us for a change, much to the general amusement. He was not stupid, obviously; he just hadn't got a clue. His mother should never have let him join the Army.

I would not like you to think that I had no respect for the officer class; on the contrary, the officers, especially the junior ones, were the backbone of the British Army, and many who I served under I considered exceptional men, especially Van Someren. But that man? Well, I suppose he might have ended up worthy of respect if his attitude had been tempered in the fire of battle.

We were well into Germany by this time. We had only a few more lengthy marches before we reached our destination. We did not march into Cologne itself; we halted at a small town about five or six miles outside – Bruhl, I think the name was. It was a few days before Christmas 1918, and as we were to make this our permanent base, there was much activity finding accommodation for everyone, establishing the cookhouse, canteen, officers' quarters and orderly room facilities.

I was allocated a billet with an old couple, who seemed rather scared at the sight of my equipment as I dumped it all on the floor. The old lady was particularly afraid of my entrenching-tool handle, of all things.

She ignored my revolver, and gingerly touching the entrenching-tool handle, she exclaimed excitedly, '*Was ist das?*' Even I understood that question, but how on earth I was going to answer her in her own language was quite another matter. So I took out the tool itself, which was carried in a kind of pouch, suspended from the waist belt at the back, and inserted the handle, thus completing the tool and then I mimed the motions of digging a trench with it. With great relief, she clasped her hands and indicated that she understood, saying, '*Ja! Ja!*'

The poor woman had thought it was a cosh. Even if it had been a cosh she would have need to be more afraid of the revolver, I would have thought. Anyway, her fears being somewhat allayed, she showed me into a little room on the ground floor containing a single bed and a few religious pictures and emblems. Everything was as clean as a new pin.

She became quite used to my comings and goings and I made a special point of trying to gain her confidence with gestures of goodwill to her and the old man. Actually, what with parades, meal times, and the like, I did not spend much time with them at all, but what little time I did spend I tried to make them feel safe and that I was not a wicked 'Englander' sent to kill them.

On my first night there, I had a very pleasant surprise. After spending the evening in the sergeants' mess, I found that my hosts had gone to bed, so I went to my little room and undressed for bed myself (for the first time in a long while, having lived and slept in my uniform). I got into bed expecting icy sheets, but I was surprised to find two old fashioned stone hot water bottles, making the bed cosy and warm. I cannot even begin to describe how delightful it was to slip into a lovely warm bed. I felt like a cat who has discovered the best armchair. And that was not all. When I had blown out the candle, I heard the old lady come downstairs. She knocked politely on the door and came in, carrying a paraffin lamp and an alarm clock. She put the alarm clock close to my face indicating that she wanted to know what time I wanted calling the next morning. I turned the hands of the clock to seven o'clock. She said '*Ja. Ja.*' as I altered the hands to the proper time again. Then she put down the clock and lamp and tucked me in! After that she picked up her lamp and clock and bade me '*Guten Nacht.*' I replied with an English 'Good night.' To tell the truth, I felt a bit of a ninny being tucked in like that, and she did it every night I was there.

The old couple were very poor, and as they were so kind to me I tried to help them with tins of bully beef and a few army biscuits now and then, or the odd tit bit from the sergeants' mess, for which they were very appreciative. Their fear of me soon vanished; indeed, I often came back in the afternoon to have a little chat with them, if 'chat' it could be called. One day the old lady asked me if I could try to obtain some chocolate for her sister who lived in a monastery. On Christmas Eve, I managed to get a half-pound slab of Cadbury's chocolate from our newly-established canteen. When I gave it to her, she could not have been more delighted if I had presented her with a diamond tiara! She indicated that she would take it to her sister the following day, Christmas Day. She had told me before, by signs and gestures, that her sister was very poor. I reckoned if she was poorer than my hosts then God help her! I understood why the Germans had had to surrender – their people were starving.

On Christmas Day we had church parade in the morning, after which we broke up for lunch, which was a frugal affair, but not for any reason of food shortage; on the contrary, we had never been so well off for food since arriving on the Western Front. We were under strength too, whilst receiving rations for a full Company, and with no 'middle men' to filch from them, we were well provided for. The reason for the frugal lunch was that the Commanding Officer had arranged for a 'spread' in the evening and arranged for officers and all other ranks to have this Christmas dinner together in a large hall, with the band playing a selection to us while we ate. (It seemed our new CO was turning up trumps after all.) We did not have turkey, but there was plenty of roast beef, pork with various sauces, plum pudding, mince pies and the rest of the trimmings. After scoffing all that, great bowls of rum-punch appeared. It was not rationed as might have been expected, so it became a 'help yourself' session.

Well, there are no prizes for guessing what happened after that. Nearly everyone got drunk. I was very merry, although still in control of myself. I did not feel the need to get drunk. For me it was no longer a case of 'eat, drink and be merry for tomorrow you may die'. 'Tomorrow' at last held some hope for the future. 'Tomorrow', I knew, there would be no sudden call to the trenches. The war was over, I had survived it, and I felt a great relief for that. I believe everyone present was conscious of a great change happening in our lives. Our old lives, which had been full of terror and dread and death, were gone; into our new lives had come peace. So who could blame us for making the most of that Christmas Day gathering – even if there were a few sore heads the next morning?

As the old year, 1918, was waning and the new one dawning, there was much speculation about demobilisation, for the majority of us had joined up for 'three years or the duration of the war'. Now that the war was ended, our period of service was over too, and we all wondered when we would be going home for good. Of course, we knew that we could not all be demobilised together, as a certain number of troops had to be retained until the peace treaty was signed, so obviously the demobilisation had to be carried out gradually. The first to go home would be men who worked in key industries, of which mining was one of the highest on the list. So, it was early in January 1919 that I heard that, as I had been a miner before the war, I would be in the first batch of men to go home.

We entrained at our local station for Cologne, where we joined other men of our Division. Our troops had obviously made a good impression on the local townspeople, because they turned out and gave us a wonderful send-off. Whether it was sincere or not, it certainly seemed so (both sides were glad the fighting was over), and we responded accordingly. At Cologne, we boarded another train consisting of one carriage (for officers); the rest of the train was cattle trucks, and considering we all carried our full kit, except firearms, we had a better deal than the officers, who had little room to lie down, whereas we could lie down comfortably. In any case, we thought, what did it matter? We would all be in Dunkirk by evening. Well, that was what we thought, little realising the kind of train we were on was not much better than Stevenson's Rocket. It seemed to have only two speeds: 'dead slow' and 'stop'. We spent two days and nights on that train, arriving at Dunkirk on the third day.

Before we reached Dunkirk, we had a fairly long stop at the town of Hazebrouck, which had once been the rail-head and main supplies centre for the whole of the British Army in Belgium and Northern France. It was busier than ever at that time, supplying the British Army on the Rhine. Our train had stopped alongside a ration train bound for the Rhine and one truck was loaded with cases of rum and guarded by a sentry. The sentry was 'engaged in conversation' by some of our boys while others liberated several cases from the other side of the truck to our train. There would have been even more cases transferred but for the fact that our train suddenly began to move, which called a halt to the operation.

Each case contained two stone bottles, each bottle holding about a gallon of rum. One case found its way into our particular cattle truck. I need to point out here that the rum which comprised our rum ration was not like the rum normally bought in public houses and off-licenses. Two tablespoons of it were enough to make most men drunk, so having two gallons of the stuff aboard was rather alarming, and anything could happen before we finally reached Dunkirk. For my part, I filled my water bottle, which held a quart (two pints), my intention being to take it home for a family celebration. Most of the men put some in their water bottles with the same intention, as we expected to be boarding the ship home that afternoon – but it was not to be.

Meanwhile, it transpired that the engine driver had grabbed an entire bottle for himself and was drinking it like beer, and, while he could still stand, he insisted on opening the throttle to full speed, ignoring all signals. He would have driven the train to destruction if not for the fireman, who fortunately had kept a level head and was able to restrain the driver and take over himself.

We did not reach Dunkirk that night (whether it was intended we stop before Dunkirk or not, I do not know), but we stopped some distance away, and we were told to get down from the train and march the last bit, across fields to a camp – which consisted of tents. Tents, in January! As we got off the train, we did not assemble in any sort of formation as there was insufficient room for that between the train and the hedgerow alongside. There was a large gap in the hedge through which we climbed. On the other side the ground was inches deep in slimy, yellow mud, which proved too much for the engine driver, who fell repeatedly into it. By this time he was fighting drunk, challenging anybody who tried to help him up to a fight; he was covered from head to foot in mud and looked like something from a horror film.

He was not the only one inebriated, though he was the only one spoiling for a fight; the others were just helpless, incapable of doing anything much except roll about in the mud. They were a pitiful sight, really.

When we reached the camp, which itself was a quagmire, the Camp Commandant sent two men with a horse-drawn dray to bring in the men who were drunk and incapable. As they came into camp, we could see the men lying across the flat bed of the dray like sardines in a tin. None appeared to be moving except by the undulations of the dray. On closer inspection, we discovered a sorry sight indeed: two of the men were not just dead drunk, they were dead. One of these men had been in the war since 1914. I found it hard to take in such a tragedy. To think that this man had probably, in his years in the trenches, escaped death by a hair's breadth scores of times, to end up like this. To my mind, it was more tragic to die like this than being killed in action, as it must also have been to his sorrowing relatives, waiting at home for their hero to return.

The potency of the rum ration was widely known, so should those men have known better? Well, Army rum, when taken properly, could be a great comfort to men in the firing line; it had been to me. A nip (about a tablespoon) would warm you up at 'stand down', a double nip before a battle for 'courage', but abused it was like a deadly poison. Throughout the war, I had rarely seen cases where the rum ration was abused; in fact I can recall only one. We had been helping take rations up the line and heard moaning coming from a derelict building. Inside we found a man clutching a rum bottle, not wounded but looking a bit sorry for himself. We decided that we would pick him up on our way back, but, by the time we returned to him it was too late, he had drunk himself to death.

So, we arrived at the camp a bit subdued. It was also very boring with little to do except walk into Dunkirk every day to see if there was a ship likely to have come for us. The camp notice-board revealed little. We inspected it optimistically every day for three very long weeks. The air in the camp became restive, even mutinous. Assistance came in the form of a Scottish Regimental Sergeant Major. Under his leadership, we formed up outside the Camp Commandant's hut and demanded that he send immediately for a ship to take us home. The RSM pointed out that we had all become thoroughly lousy again because of the filthy blankets in the tents, and that the men were in danger of developing trench foot through lack of whale oil and the muddy conditions which had made the insides of the tents as bad as the outside. The RSM was not abusive or rude to the CC but he made his point nevertheless, letting the CC know that trouble was brewing and something needed to happen soon to allow the men to go home. It worked. There was a ship for us two days later.

Our crossing was uneventful and after another railway journey we arrived back at Harrowby Camp in Grantham to receive our demobilisation papers. Our reputation had obviously gone before us, for as we formed a long queue at the desk where two officers were issuing the demob papers, another officer and sergeant walked along the line muttering disparaging remarks and reminding us that we were not out of the Army yet, so we had better watch it! Not one of us dared answer back, much as we would have like to have strangled that sergeant.

We eventually got our demobilisation papers (I was passed as A1 fit – no mean achievement after nearly three years in the trenches) and rushed to look up the train times from a list on the notice-board. Then, the sergeant came up to us and said, 'If any of you are thinking of catching the next train to Birmingham, forget it! It is for officers only.' We even stood for that. With freedom in our pockets it would have been so easy to have punched him one, but then we would probably have been detained for it. So we ignored him and let it pass, and the six of us for Birmingham, irrespective of what our dear sergeant had just said, went to wait for the next Birmingham train. We half expected the station master to tell us the incoming train was 'for officers only', but he did not, so we jumped in and heaved an enormous sigh of relief as it pulled out of the station.

I had not been able to let my family know the exact day of my homecoming, and I had not heard from them for some time, so my eventual arrival was something of a surprise. It was just getting dusk when I walked into Church Street, Bloxwich – and there was not a soul in sight! But news travels fast, and it was not long before the whole street was bedecked with flags, a tribute which was accorded to every returning serviceman as he came home to Church Street. Other streets did the same, of course.

So, it was February 1919 and I was back in the family fold at last, and a free man. Free? Yes, but only 99 per cent 'free'. I had been, as all the others had been too, 'Transferred to Army Reserve'. Technically speaking I was still in the Army, as I had not been finally discharged; in fact, I was *never* finally discharged – but I think it's a bit late now. They probably wouldn't want me at 77.

CHAPTER THIRTEEN

BACK TO BLIGHTY – MARRIAGE – AUSTRALIA

Back home at last – and what a wonderful feeling it was! No more the deadly whine of bullets or the ground-shaking blasts of high explosives. No more the threat of being blown to pieces at any second, or blinded by gas shells, or choked by phosgene, or any one of the other countless dangers I had encountered in the insane war which had just ended.

Physically I had left all that behind in Belgium and France, but mentally the war was still very much with me. No-one can witness such things – the destruction, the relentless cacophony of shells, and the daily, pointless, bloody slaughter of young men, lose friends and comrades all the time knowing it could be your turn next – and not remain affected by it. I thought I would never get the stench of those battlefields out of my nostrils, or the pitiful cries of the dying and wounded out of my head. Many times during the ensuing years, I would dream such terrible nightmares that I would wake up crying out and drenched with sweat. When realisation came that I was safe at home and they were only dreams I would feel so thankful that any other troubles seemed insignificant by comparison.

So, it was nothing short of glorious to be home with my family and friends, to begin living a normal life again and able to look forward to a happy future. It felt wonderful to have survived it all. My brother Edgar, who had been serving with the Royal Navy, was also on his way home. There was sadness too; my brother Tom wasn't going to be returning, having lost his life in 1917.

It was once I was home that I had time to consider all that I had been through, and what I had survived. I was glad to be alive – literally. Considering the millions upon millions of projectiles which had been hurled in both directions, with hardly an inch of ground being missed, it seemed truly miraculous that anyone came back alive. I had been on the Western Front for nearly three years, for most of that time on the front line, in some of the bloodiest battles in one of the bloodiest wars. I had seen countless friends and comrades die. The casualties had been enormous – I believe over 750,000 British troops died, not to mention the millions wounded – and yet I had managed to survive it intact. How I did it, I do not know, but I thanked God for it!

On arriving back home, as soon as circumstances permitted, my chief aim was to take a bath and dispose of all my vermin-infested underclothing. I was appalled to discover that although I had started my return journey from Cologne with two sets of new, clean under-clothing, I had arrived home wearing one completely infested set, with the other, similarly infested, in my pack. Fortunately, the lice didn't seem to infest our outer clothes, only clothes worn next to the body, so my tunic and trousers were not so bad. Neither did they infect the hair; only the warmest parts of the body. The lice disgusted me and I couldn't wait to get the bath brought in and wash myself clean.

After my bath I changed into my pre-war civilian clothes, and Ada made short work of the underclothes by burning them under the boiler. My uniform she hung outside on the clothes line and gave it a good bashing – just in case. Only then did I feel clean once more. I was allowed to keep my uniform, as we all were, of course. We could either keep our greatcoats or hand them in and receive a pound for it. I handed mine in. This brought up the total of my 'bounty' on leaving the Army to £21.

'Bounty' was based on rank and service. My bounty as a sergeant with a total of nearly three years and four months' service was consid-ered generous. A private with the same service would have received only thirteen or fourteen pounds, plus the pound for his greatcoat. I remember at the time reading the list in the newspapers of what the generals and senior officers received – it was like reading a millionaire's will. Thousands of pounds, titles, big houses. The government called this 'gratuity'; the soldiers called it 'blood money'. What the generals and 'high-ups' called it I don't know, but I should think they called it 'money for old rope'. Many soldiers like myself felt disgusted by it, and more than a little betrayed. This was no way to treat 'returning heroes'.

However, my home town did put on a bit of a 'do' for their 'returning heroes'. I had my picture in the local paper and received a write-up in the *Walsall Observer* of 22 March 1919.

THREE BLOXWICH HEROES

Mayor Attends Discharged Men's Federation Meeting

On Monday evening a procession of Service and ex-Service men formed at the Swan Inn, High Street, Bloxwich ... and headed by the Bloxwich Imperial Prize Band, paraded the principal streets before meeting at the Central Hall (kindly lent by Councillor Pat Collins) where, before a large and very enthusiastic audience, the Mayor (Councillor A J Llewellen) presented three medals won by Bloxwich men during the war. The recipients were Corporal Knowles, 17, Bell Lane, Bloxwich, D.C.M.; Lance-corporal Cartwright, 8, Old Lane, Bloxwich, M.M.; and Sergeant Rowbotham, 60, Church Street, Bloxwich, M.M., and each man also received a small monetary gift ...

(The 'small monetary gift' must have indeed been small, because I can't recall receiving it, but I suppose it was better than a kick in the backside.)

The official accounts of the deeds which gained these Bloxwich heroes their awards, and which were read out by the Mayor, are as follows.

IN AT THE DEATH

Sgt E. Rowbotham, Machine Gun Corps, enlisted on November 1st 1915 and went out to France on March 10th 1916. He was at Ypres for five months, and took part in the third battle, fought for three months on the

Somme, and took part in the great British offensive in July 1916, was in the attack on Cambrai on November 20th 1917, and in the retirement from the Ypres Salient in April last year. He won the Military Medal on August 8–9, during an attack on Hill 44 when 'by gallantry and devotion to duty, although wounded, he remained in command of a machine gun.' He was in the last battle of the war, Landrecies, on November 4th, and after marching to the Rhine, was demobilised on January 10th …

The Mayor was obliged to leave immediately after the presentation, but was accorded a vote of thanks …

Well, it wasn't much of a 'do', and the Mayor did scarper pretty sharpish as soon as he'd pinned on the medals, but it was a lot more than many 'returning heroes' had.

So, I was back home in one piece after three years living and fighting inside the gates of Hell and, as you might expect of a young man deprived of female company for that time, my thoughts very soon turned to love – or Miss Lily Totty, to be precise. Lily was the sister of Phoebe Collingswood who kept the off-licence in Church Street, two doors away from our house. If you remember, I had asked Lily to write to me while I was in the trenches and we had been corresponding regularly since then. Lily had been one of my teenage 'flames' and in our mutual correspondence we had renewed our former regard for each other. We were both the same age within a week or so, and when we first became acquainted I thought she was the most lovely being ever born. She was very beautiful, but she was also something of a flirt, which was why we had drifted apart. I thought that as we were both older and more mature now, I might take a chance (that is, jump in with both my big feet) and ask her to be my fiancée. It was an impetuous thing to do, but I suppose, in the aftermath of the war, I wasn't always thinking straight.

She was in service at a hotel in Martineau Street in Birmingham, where I went to visit her. I had not informed her of my visit, so I turned up at the hotel and asked for Miss Totty at the reception desk where, in normal circumstances, I should have been told to go to the tradesmen's entrance, but I was in uniform, which made all the difference, as I was a returning 'hero', and so I was respectfully escorted through the hotel to the kitchen. There were other girls with her in the kitchen, and as I looked around I spotted Lily and went straight up to her, grabbed her, and gave her a resounding kiss full on the lips. She blushed to the roots of her hair, much to the amusement of the other girls, who all stopped working and watched us in amazement: kissing in public in those days was normally frowned upon by the older generation, and usually reserved for the front parlour. But those girls were all young and I think they quite enjoyed the unrehearsed spectacle.

When poor Lily had recovered from the shock, we adjourned to the hotel yard for a little chat, the outcome of which was that she agreed to become my girl. Had I been four weeks later coming home, I would have missed her as she had already given a month's notice to take up a post in Hove, near Brighton. During those four weeks we saw quite a lot of each other. I went to see her three times a week, when we would ride on the train into the suburbs and find a quiet spot for a tête-à-tête. She was so beautiful and it was not difficult to fall in love with her all over again.

I urged her not to take up the new post, but she was determined to try it out for a few months at least. She said that if it was not all she expected then she would come back. She promised to save up all her time off so that she could have several days together so we could spend them with each other. So she went, and we kept up a regular correspondence. We agreed to become engaged on her first vacation.

This vacation came in the early summer of 1919, but on the day before she was due to come back to Bloxwich, I received an anonymous letter, from one of her colleagues presumably, who signed herself 'a friend'. In the letter she said how she hated to see anyone deceived and thought it only right that I should know how Miss Totty was behaving in the hotel. According to this 'friend', Lily was having an affair with an elderly resident of the hotel – she went into some detail about it. The letter left me in a quandary: whether to completely ignore it – it could have just been malicious – or to have it out with Lily when I saw her the next day. I decided to have it out with her.

So, the next day, Lily and I found ourselves sitting on a park bench in a secluded part of Handsworth Park, which might have been idyllic for us under normal conditions. After a little while, I drew the letter from my pocket, saying at the same time, 'I've had this letter from someone in your hotel. I think you ought to read it.'

As she began to read it, I was watching her face, in hope rather than condemnation, to observe her reaction. It was not reassuring. She went very quiet for a few seconds, then she said, 'I know who wrote that! Wait till I get back, she'll get a piece of my mind!' She made no attempt to deny it; she seemed more concerned at having been found out. At least, that was how it seemed to me. I was very worried and did not want to lose her, but I could feel that already a gulf had opened up between us, and in an effort to close it I said, 'Lily, *I'm* not accusing you of anything. It's the letter that accuses you, not me.' Then I added, 'Please tell me it's not true and I'll believe you.'

'Of course it isn't true,' she answered, trying to look indignant. 'I'm surprised at you, Ted, believing an anonymous letter rather than me.'

It was a little unconvincing, perhaps, but I was so anxious not to quarrel with her that I was ready to believe her. So, I put my arm around her and said, 'Come on, let's forget all about it.'

She seemed ill at ease for a little while, but eventually we made arrangements for her to come to tea at my home the following day (Sunday). She would come over to Bloxwich, then stay the night at Phoebe Collingswood's house, two doors away. I had arranged to take the day off work on the Monday so that we could go to Walsall together to choose an engagement ring. We parted on the Saturday night on much better terms, and with a final kiss and a hug I went home with a sense of relief that I had cleared up the matter of the anonymous letter.

On the Sunday afternoon I was to meet her off the tram at the King's Arms tram stop in Bloxwich at three o'clock. I was down there well before three o'clock, watching every tram that came up from Walsall. Meanwhile, my sisters Ada, Hilda and Gertie were preparing the tea, which was to be a 'spread' worthy of the occasion of my engagement. Well, I paced up and down near the King's Arms up until five-thirty, when I gave up and went home. The celebration tea my sisters had so painstakingly prepared was something of a flop, to say the least, but, ever the optimist, even while I was eating it, I kept thinking of several eventualities that may have prevented her from coming. However, in my heart, I knew the real reason.

I did not go to work on the Monday morning; I still hoped she might come and we could go and buy the ring and everything would be alright. She did not, however, and during the day I received a letter from her. She said she had come to the conclusion that if I could not trust her then I was not good enough for her. And, if she made friends with rich old men in the hotel then that was her affair! Which I suppose said it all. And that, you won't be surprised to hear, was the end of my love affair with Lily Totty.

Unlucky in love I might have been but at least I was lucky in finding a job. By the time I received my bounty from the Army I had started to work again, in a pit called 'The Struggling Monkey' – the proper name for which was The Broad Lane Colliery Company Ltd. It felt a bit strange at first, having been away from the work for so long – I suppose the war had changed me – and it took a little while to get back into the routine. The wages were good and I soon began to save a little money each week. Now, I have never been a compulsive saver; in fact, my family will tell you it is more the opposite! Money, to me, has always been something to be used, and up to the time of my demobilisation I was never able to save more than a pound or two – and anyway, savings wouldn't have been much use to me if I'd been blown to pieces. But now the war was ended and I was looking forward to married life with Lily, I suddenly felt it was incumbent on me to save what I could.

About that time, Percy Eagleton, the Australian corporal who had married my sister Nellie, was also demobbed, and they both lived with us in Church Street for a short time, after which they went to live in Pimlico in London to await repatriation to Australia. I visited them in Pimlico several times and, on one of these occasions, I remembered an address of the parents of a certain Private Mulcaster, who had belonged to my gun team and had been killed in action in 1917. When I had sent home their son's effects, among which was a cigarette case with a bullet hole through it (the bullet had been the fatal one), I received a reply to the effect that if I was ever in London I was to be sure to look them up and, if possible, give them some details of their son's death. On showing Percy their address he explained that it was only a tuppenny tram ride from Pimlico. So there and then I decided to go.

It was a Sunday afternoon and, on finding the address, I knocked on the door, which was opened by a big, burly fellow. 'Mr Mulcaster?' I enquired.

'Yes!' answered the man.

'My name's Rowbotham, and I was your son's sergeant in the Machine Gun Corps.'

'Come in! Come in, Sergeant!' he replied. 'I'm very glad to see you. You're very welcome.' And he ushered me into the living room.

Even though I was not in uniform he continued to call me 'Sergeant'. He seemed a nice chap, which belied my first impression of him when he had opened the door to me. We talked of many things but particularly of his son's death. He still had the cigarette case through which the deadly bullet had passed, and it was obvious that his son had been, and still was, very dear to him. It had been over two years since his son had been killed, so the first terrible pangs of bereavement were dulled, and he could talk fondly of him.

We gradually drifted into general conversation, during which he disclosed that he was a police detective. He proceeded to recount several amusing stories of his activities. He was very interested in my occupation as a miner and pressed me to explain something about pit work as he had never met a miner before.

He made me stay for tea, and he put on a splendid spread, which I thought was quite a feat for a man living on his own – he and his wife were living apart and he was obviously lonely. After tea, he insisted we go out for a walk. He was very amusing with his remarks about different places where he had made this or that arrest. I was really enjoying myself. Suddenly, we found ourselves approaching a public house and, as we reached the door, he stopped and whispered, 'Listen!' As we listened we could hear the hubbub going on inside – a proper racket. Then he said, 'Now, see how quiet it goes when they see me.'

How right he was! The talking stopped just as if it had been switched off as soon as he stepped inside. As he ordered us some drinks I could feel many pairs of eyes on me. I mentioned this to my companion who said, 'They're wondering who you are. They know you aren't tall enough to be a policeman and they're puzzled as to whether you're an informer.' He said that they would never believe he might be with a friend, because in his job he didn't make many friends. I could tell he was lonely; when we left the pub he even saw me to my tram stop.

I enjoyed staying with Nellie and Perce. Talking to Perce, I became very impressed with his descriptions of Australia, so much so that I made up my mind that when I got married my bride and I would emigrate there under the free passage scheme which had been inaugurated by the two respective governments. The bride I had in mind, of course, was Lily Totty, who I thought I was about to become engaged to, little knowing what was to come. Well, the best laid plans, and all that, and my plans for Lily Totty certainly went 'agley'.

I did go to Australia though, and arrived there in January 1921, but with a different bride. I was married in 1920 to Edie Parton, an old friend of the family and a widow. In former days, she and her husband used to often visit us in Church Street and were always welcome. There was a slight connection in relationship with Edie and Bill Parton and our family, as my brother Ernie had married Bill's sister, Sarah. Edie Parton (née Foxall) had suffered a triple tragedy during the flu epidemic of 1918/19 when not only Bill but also her two baby boys had died. She was deeply affected by her loss, although she would never talk about it. After Bill and her boys died, Edie stopped coming to our house, until I happened to meet her on a tram going from Walsall to Bloxwich one Saturday afternoon. I remember she was still dressed in mourning, although Bill had been dead some time. I asked her why she had stopped visiting us and she answered that she didn't think she would be as welcome if Bill wasn't with her. I told her she would be as welcome as ever. So, she began visiting regularly again. My Dad was pleased too; we all were. It was like one of the family returning to the fold.

Now, to suggest at that stage that I might have entertained any amorous feelings towards Edie would be wrong. At the time I still had not got Lily out of my system. But, eventually Lily began to fade and Edie began to rise in my estimation. I suddenly began to look on her with different eyes. She was a desirable woman and excellent company. Yes, I was falling in love – again! So, one Wednesday night when she had come to visit us, I proposed to her and she accepted. Then I told her my plans for going to Australia, and, to my delight, she assured me she would go anywhere in the world with me. I remember feeling so happy at the prospect, and we made arrangements to meet again the following Sunday night.

On the morning after my proposal to Edie, I was talking to Dad, when suddenly he said, 'It's time you settled down, Ted, lad. Why don't you make it up with Edie Parton? She's a nice wench.'

'That's a coincidence, Dad,' said I, 'I proposed to her last night.'

'Good,' said Dad, 'I'm glad. You're nearly 29. It's time you met somebody worthwhile.'

His comment said a lot about his opinion of my romantic attachments to date, didn't it?

I felt strangely secure with Edie. We both lived within a mile or so of each other, so we could meet regularly, and did not have to do our courting by correspondence as had been the case with both Agnes and Lily. At last, it seemed I had found 'the one'.

It was a coincidence that on that first Sunday night I was to meet Edie as my 'girl', I was to encounter Lily first. Lily was on one of her periodic visits and staying with her sister Phoebe at the off-licence. She seemed to spend a lot of time standing on the doorstep, according to information which came to me from various members of the family, who would say to me at varying times of the day, 'Lily's on the doorstep, Ted.' I must admit, I had the urge several times to go out to her and have a word, but something stopped me. For once, I think, I let myself be ruled by my head rather than my heart. Besides, I knew I had to consider Edie.

I found myself comparing the two women. While Lily was endowed with a beauty that was fascinating and lovely, she had little else to offer. Edie, on the other hand, was lively and jolly, honest and straightforward, and not given to flirtation. She was smart and good looking. Also her background was the same as mine – working class. Lily's background I always considered to be different – *upper* working class, I suppose you could say. She was the youngest of a family of ten sisters, all very beautiful women, some of whom had married into money and were quite wealthy. I could understand Lily's attraction then to the elderly gentleman in the hotel, as her desire to do the same. She was never likely to be rich married to me.

On Sunday evening I got myself done up to go to Walsall to meet Edie, and on coming out at the bottom of our entry I had to walk past the off-licence, and guess what? Lily was on the doorstep. I had to think quickly, whether to stop or pass straight on. In the few steps it took me to reach her I had decided not to stop. I just said a quick hello and hurried on my way, conscious of having won a victory over myself. That was the last time we ever met, which was perhaps a good thing, for her with her Rolls Royce tastes and me with my Flivver prospects, our union would have produced nothing but trouble. (A Flivver, incidentally, was a cheap motor car.)

So, I went to meet Edie as arranged, and from then on we met and enjoyed each other's company regularly. We became officially engaged and eventually got married in Blakenall Church on 19 January 1920. My brother Albert was best man, the chief bridesmaid was a cousin of mine from Birmingham, Florence Murphy – her mother was my mother's sister. I recall that the ceremony went very well, and as the sun was shining, there were quite a few people outside waiting to pelt us with rice and confetti. I cannot recall exactly what my bride wore, or the bridesmaids, or even what I wore myself, but I do remember quite clearly that I provided a lovely splash of colour with a huge red pimple on the end of my nose.

The wedding celebration was of the usual sort with plenty to eat and drink, and socialising with relatives and friends of both families, sizing each other up and generally being convivial. In those days working people did not have honeymoons – just a great binge and then another day off to 'regain composure', then back to work.

It was very amusing on coming home to my new bride after my first day at work in the pit as a married man. Although Edie had been a visitor to our family for many years, she was not really familiar with a miner's appetite. Her father and brothers were all factory workers and were able to have their main meal ('dinner') during the midday break, unlike miners underground who were only able to have a snack to sustain them between breakfast and home-time, so ate a substantial meal in the evening; in other words, miners had their 'dinner' at 'tea time'. This gave rise, in Edie's mind at least, having seen our evening meals at Church Street, that miners had two dinners, and therefore possessed unusually large appetites.

Therefore, the meal she had prepared for me was vast, an immense pile of meat and vegetables on an enormous plate. As I tucked into it, I knew I had to say something.

'I can't eat all this, Edie.'

'Why, Ted? Isn't it nice?'

'It's lovely,' I replied, 'but there's too much.'

'I thought miners had big appetites.'

'There's enough here for two men.'

I think she must have thought I was joking, because she just smiled and said, 'Well, eat up, then. I'm going to sit here until you've finished the lot.'

This was only our second day of married bliss and, in order to please my new bride, I strived manfully to finish off the pile of food. I eventually accomplished it, after which I had a belly like a harvest frog, and felt uncomfortable for hours afterwards.

The same procedure went on for two or three evenings after that. I have always had a healthy appetite, but Edie's dinners were enough to tax the appetite of a man twice my size. They made me so uncomfortable that I knew I had to say something about it, but was at a loss as to how to tell her. On the third or fourth evening, we sat at the table with another gigantic portion in front of me. I just could not eat it.

Suddenly, I put my knife and fork down on the plate and pushed it gently aside, leaving at least a quarter of the food untouched.

'What's the matter?' she asked in alarm. 'Aren't you well?'

'Never better,' I answered. 'But I've had enough, and enough is as good as a feast.'

'But you must eat,' she said.

'Not this time,' I answered, clutching my aching stomach. 'Look, this is my belly, and I'm the lad who knows when it's full.'

She called me a 'miserable article' (Edie always had a good repertoire of interesting phrases), but I could see she had got the message, and I was grateful, because I much preferred being a miserable article to being dead from overeating. Anyway, she forgave me, and we ended up in each other's arms, which was just as it should be.

At that time, Edie was working as a saddle-stitcher in a Walsall factory called Jabez-Cliff. Walsall had a thriving leather industry then; it still has as I write these memoirs. Now that I was earning enough to be the sole breadwinner, I suggested she could give up her job. This may sound unreasonable to people today, but you must bear in mind the different customs of this period. In the 1920s, the day to day lives of the people were still very much influenced by the social conventions of the Victorian and Edwardian eras. It was true that after the war, certain things were changing, but still, old customs die hard.

It was a superstition, for example, among miners, that if a man saw a woman on his way to work, it meant that something bad would happen during the day. The superstition was so strong in some mining communities that men would turn round and go home again. Of course, it was understandable that miners should be superstitious, as accidents down the pit were very common, and due to the nature of their work miners often had their own codes of behaviour, one of which was that it was acceptable for a single girl to go out to work, but not a married woman. Any man who allowed his wife to go to work was either a man disabled by accident or illness, or he was not 'man enough' to earn sufficient money to keep her, in which case he would be subjected to many wry glances and snide remarks from his contemporaries.

I was in vigorous health and well able to keep us both, so you can understand that I resented the wry glances *I* received, and I soon shut up anyone who dared to make disparaging remarks about my wife working. All the same, I kept asking Edie to give up her job. She finally relented the following Easter. I suppose today it might be called 'macho' stupidity, but I felt under social pressure to obey the code. But we were the losers, because the money Edie earned would have been very useful in our preparations for our emigration to Australia.

Our plans to emigrate were going ahead. There was much to do in regard to passports, photographs, medical examinations and what have you, and although the passage to Australia was free for ex-servicemen, we would have to travel in separate parts of the ship, men in their own quarters, women and children in theirs. We did not like this idea, so I enquired about a private cabin for two which, in the end, we obtained by paying for it. It cost around twenty pounds if I remember rightly, which seemed a lot, but well worth it for the privacy it afforded us on the long voyage.

When we had put all our affairs in order I left my job at the pit, and we set off on our adventure. We eventually sailed from Tilbury docks on 2 December 1920 on the SS *Beltana*. We had been accompanied as far as London by Albert and his wife, Nellie, but no visitors were allowed on the boat train to Tilbury, so we made our farewells on the platform. It was a fond farewell, and I, for my part, felt very sorry to leave them behind as I thought what a rosy future lay ahead for Edie and I, while poor Albert and Nellie were to stay behind in England, which I (and many others at that time) thought was on the verge of ruin.

I thought what a tragedy it was that after losing nearly a million dead and millions wounded and disabled that there was no employment for those who came through it. Where were the men who had promised to make the country fit for heroes to live in? What had become of Lloyd George's dream of 'three acres and a cow' for every ex-serviceman who wanted it? The promises had been empty ones and the dreams had not materialised, and I really did believe Britain, the country I and so many others had fought for, was heading for ruin. I couldn't think what on earth was to become of all the loved ones we were leaving behind.

Little did I know how wrong I was. It seems to me now, looking back over the years, that this country has always been on the verge of ruin. Even today, in this year of 1967, there is much concern about our scientists all leaving the country; also our technicians, engineers and doctors leaving in their thousands: it's called the 'brain drain'. There are still people dying needlessly in wars started by politicians. There are still the 'haves' and the 'have nots'. So, today's government is no better than Asquith's or Lloyd George's – now it is Wilson's turn to run us all to disaster! When we have a government that is not ruining the country then, I suppose, we shall have reached Utopia.

So, in the early afternoon of that December day, the ship SS *Beltana* began to move slowly down the Thames estuary. The rails all around the ship were lined with emigrants taking a last long look at the old country, many of them (myself included) wondering if we would ever see old Blighty again.

EPILOGUE

That was my Grandad's story – but not the end of it, of course.

Returning to normal life was not easy for him – and countless other ex-soldiers who had 'survived' the horrors of the Great War. He quickly became disillusioned with life in Britain after the war and, with the Depression looming, he emigrated to Australia with his new bride in December 1920 in search of a better life. Sadly, he didn't find one.

He made his home in the small mining town of Wonthaggi, south-east of Melbourne, and worked in the coal mines there. In September 1921 his wife, Edie, gave birth to their daughter, Edith – their only child. The birth of her daughter made Edie yearn for home; in fact, they were both homesick for their families, and life in Australia was not the Utopia Grandad was searching for. Pit work was hard there, and the pay no better than back home.

It was while Grandad was in Wonthaggi that he had another one of his 'ideas': he invented a device which was still in use in pits all over the world at the time he wrote his memoirs. It should have made him a very rich man. The invention itself was very simple: it was a specially designed drill 'bit' with cutting edges which enabled the operator to drill a hole (for blasting) twice as fast as the existing equipment. It also had the advantage of being detachable from the end of the drill, which meant that only the 'bit' had to be taken away and carried to the surface for sharpening instead of the whole set of drills which weighed over twenty pounds. It was simple but quite brilliant, designed to save both time and work for the miners, and therefore, as they were on piece work, make more money for them. Naturally, it would make more money for the mine *owners* too.

He even patented his invention (or thought he had) and tried to sell the rights to a big American company operating in Australia. Sadly, the patent agent, probably sensing the money to be made from such a device, colluded with the American company, who were determined to get their hands on it for free. Grandad's lack of business acumen made him an easy target to be conned, and his invention was stolen. His dreams of being a rich man were dashed.

Then, in 1926, there was a rumour that the Wonthaggi mines were closing, and Grandad decided it was time to sell up and go home. He sold his house for £360 and sailed for England – where he found 'dear old Blighty' slap bang in the middle of the General Strike.

Determined to find work of some kind and make a living to support his wife and young child, he bought a lorry and tried, but failed, to set up a haulage business. There followed several fairly low paid jobs, but he seemed unable to truly settle to anything for long, which, although he might not have realised it himself, was almost certainly a legacy of his experiences in the war. It was very common: the war changed people. In truth, no-one could have witnessed the harrowing sights he and his comrades had seen on a daily basis throughout the war and *not* be changed by them.

He eventually sold his lorry and went to work as a delivery driver for J and J Wiggins in Bloxwich for two pounds ten shillings a week. After five years he could stand it no longer and moved, in 1938, to work at Bloxwich Golf Club as a mechanic for two pounds fifteen shillings a week – a job where he was the most settled and happy since the war. He was working outside, which he loved, and could work to his own timetable, this freedom being the most important to him. He mowed the greens and repaired the machinery and his proudest boast was that he succeeded in keeping the golf course playable throughout the whole of the Second World War. At the same time, of course, he was doing his duty to his country again by serving in the Home Guard. Unlike the First World War, he hated his time with the Home Guard intensely. There was no comradeship, and although during the First World War he had been promoted (deservedly) to sergeant, and had a distinguished record for his service with the Machine Gun Corps, in the Home Guard he was only made a corporal. He regarded it as a kick in the teeth.

He worked at Bloxwich Golf Club until 1947, when new management came in and imposed new methods of working. He disagreed with these methods and so he started looking around for another job. He had been seeing adverts for some time for ex-miners to go back into the pits. There was plenty of work and coal there; at the age of 57 he left the golf club and went underground once more as a fitter-mechanic at Mid Cannock Colliery, the pit he had left in 1915 to join the Army. How he missed the open air! It took him a long while to get used to it again. However, he liked the comradeship which existed between the men underground. He was affectionately known to the others as 'Ode Ted'.

He worked at Mid Cannock until his retirement in 1955 at the age of 65. His pension was one pound a week. By this time, his daughter Edith (who married in 1946) had presented him, to his delight, with two grandchildren, Sheila, born in 1950, and me (Janet) born in 1955. He threw himself wholeheartedly into both retirement and grandfa-ther-hood. He could never be still: he grew wonderful vegetables on his allotment and in his greenhouse (the best yellow tomatoes in the world!) and was always busy in his shed 'inventing' things (he never gave up hope of being a rich man). He made fantastic kites out of odd bits of wood and waxed paper and he took Sheila and me to fly them on Cannock Chase. He even invented a musical instrument, which we named 'The Thing' (it was the only way to describe it). It was a curious mixture of piano keyboard and guitar strings, and we played beautiful songs on it, if a little out of tune.

He never lost his love for playing the organ, and he never did learn to read music, but he could play anything by ear after hearing it once. He used to play for us whenever we visited; he wouldn't let us go home without playing for us. 'Shall we have a tune before you go?' he would say. His favourites were always the marches which had inspired him during the war. 'It's a Long Way to Tipperary' and 'Colonel Bogey' still bring a tear to my eye.

He acquired the daftest dog ever, Rex, who he adored. 'Rex is almost human. Speech is the only faculty he lacks,' Grandad would say fondly. Well, they say love is blind, and it was, because Rex, had he actually been human, would certainly have been confined to an asylum.

The overriding memories of my childhood, however, are of Grandad's wonderful stories. If I close my eyes I can see him now, sitting in his armchair (his retirement present from the pit, together with a pipe) swathed in clouds of noxious tobacco smoke (the blacker the tobacco the better: another legacy of his war years), regaling Sheila and me with his tales of his time in the Army. We thought how brave he was to have lived through such horrific experiences. He would always make us laugh with his lovely dry sense of humour and we would ask him over again to tell the story of the mutton fat and plum jam pudding and the time he set fire to his greatcoat. As I have been typing Grandad's reminiscences from his hand-written memoirs, I have come upon these stories and others again like meeting old friends.

He never did find Utopia, but he was always grateful for what he had, and always made the best of things. He used to say what a great comfort it was to him to have such a loving family around him in his old age. He had a long and happy retirement, remaining as fit as a fiddle, and he retained his quite extraordinary zest for living until illness finally claimed his life. Like the old soldier he was, he fought his last battle with stomach cancer courageously and without complaint. He never once gave up hope that he would win his fight. But sadly it was not to be. He died on 17 January 1973 at the age of 82.

All the old Tommies have gone now, but one old Tommy will never truly be gone – within the pages of his memoirs Edward Rowbotham lives forever.

Janet Tucker

INDEX

Visit our website and discover thousands of other History Press books.

www.thehistorypress.co.uk